本书为南京航空航天大学研究生教育教学研究改革项目(2017YJXGG19)及江苏省研究生教育教学改革课题项目(JGLX18_006)成果,获得南京航空航天大学"十三五"重点教材建设项目(90YQJ18037)基金资助。

非英语专业研究生
学术英语写作指南

A Guide to English Academic Writing
For Non-English Major Graduates

编著 陆 红

苏州大学出版社

图书在版编目(CIP)数据

学术英语写作指南:非英语专业研究生 = A Guide to English Academic Writing for Non-English Major Graduates / 陆红编著. —苏州:苏州大学出版社,2020.3
ISBN 978-7-5672-3066-8

Ⅰ.①学… Ⅱ.①陆… Ⅲ.①英语-写作-研究生-教学参考资料 Ⅳ.①H319.36

中国版本图书馆 CIP 数据核字(2019)第 289559 号

书 名:	非英语专业研究生 学术英语写作指南 A Guide to English Academic Writing for Non-English Major Graduates	
编 著:	陆 红	
责任编辑:	汤定军	
策划编辑:	汤定军	
封面设计:	刘 俊	
出版发行:	苏州大学出版社(Soochow University Press)	
社 址:	苏州市十梓街 1 号 邮编:215006	
印 装:	丹阳兴华印务有限公司	
网 址:	www.sudapress.com	
E - mail:	tangdingjun@suda.edu.cn	
邮购热线:	0512-67480030	
销售热线:	0512-67481020	
开 本:	787 mm×960 mm 1/16 印张:10.25 字数:163 千	
版 次:	2020 年 3 月第 1 版	
印 次:	2020 年 3 月第 1 次印刷	
书 号:	ISBN 978-7-5672-3066-8	
定 价:	48.00 元	

凡购本社图书发现印装错误,请与本社联系调换。服务热线:0512-67481020

前言

《学术英语写作指南：非英语专业研究生》是为初涉学术英语论文写作的硕博研究生编著的一本简明写作手册，亦可作为非英语专业本科生的学术英语写作教材。

编著者经过多年的教学观察、问卷调查和对部分学生的访谈，发现研究生科研任务较重，没有太多时间来研究写作理论。面对厚重的写作教材，学生的内心是抗拒的。而另一方面学生写作能力并没有得到加强，我们的写作教学也没有给予他们足够的实际运用机会。因此，本书将注重以下两个方面：

1. 简述写作理论，便于学生快速理解并掌握最基本的知识。

2. 坚持以任务式学习为主导思想，强调"做中学"（learning by doing），强化写作技巧。

本书共七个单元：第一、二、三单元主要介绍了学术英语论文的语言特点，编著者认为学术写作的核心能力是学术语言的运用。了解学术文体的语言风格和特点，包括学术词汇的抽象性、句子的复杂性以及段落的逻辑性，对于从宏观到微观的具体论文写作，具有十分重要的意义。第四、五、六、七单元分别讨论了论文主要部分的写作：引言、方法、结果、讨论以及摘要。大多数学生对于学术论文的程式规范已经非常了解，但在实际写作中他们仍然是先想好或写好中文再翻译成英文，写作过程复杂，学生感觉痛苦，写作结果很难令人满意。因此，本书的这四个部分着重指导学生如何灵活使用基本的学术英语句型，并学会用英文搭建论文每部分结构。

本书的主要特点在于：每个单元分为两个部分，分别围绕 What 和 How 两大问题开展。对于 What 的问题，编著者利用思维导图（Mindmap）直观地简述基本概念、理论知识,并导入样文进行阅读活动,以帮助学生快速有效地掌握基本的理论知识。第二部分是关于How的问题,编著者针对实际写作的每一个步骤,给出了详细写作技巧、句子结构以及段落模型,之后要求学生完成一到三个相关任务。学生通过即时练,加强巩固学术英语写作技能。此外,编著者在练习中有意识地增加中英互译练习,帮助学生更深刻地理解中英思维之间的差异,撰写符合学术规范的地道英文,提升跨文化学术交流意识。

  在本书编写过程中,编著者参阅了许多相关著作、教材和学术论文,谨向各位作者致以真诚的谢意。同时也感谢梁砾文博士审阅全稿并给本书提出了许多宝贵的修改意见!本书的编写也得到了南京航空航天大学外国语学院的各位同仁的大力支持,在此表示衷心感谢!

  由于编著者水平有限,加上时间仓促,书中必然存在许多不足,敬请同行和读者批评指正。

编著者
2019年8月于南京

Contents

Unit 1 Writing Academically / 1
1. What is academic writing? / 1
   - 1.1 Introduction / 1
   - 1.2 A well-structured academic research paper / 2
   - 1.3 Reading activity / 2
2. How do we write academically? / 3
   - 2.1 Using academic words / 3
   - 2.2 Using nominalization / 5
   - 2.3 Writing formally / 6
   - 2.4 Writing concisely / 7
   - 2.5 Avoiding plagiarism / 8
     - 2.5.1 APA in-text citations—direct (quotations) and indirect citations / 8
     - 2.5.2 APA reference style / 13

Unit 2 Forming an Effective Academic Sentence / 18
1. What is a sentence? / 18
   - 1.1 Introduction / 18
   - 1.2 A tree-like English sentence / 18
   - 1.3 Reading activity / 20
2. How do we form an effective academic sentence? / 22
   - 2.1 Expanding sentences with noun phrases (NPs) / 22

2.2　Writing correct sentences　/ 26
    2.2.1　Subject-verb agreements　/ 26
    2.2.2　Pronoun-antecedent agreements　/ 27
    2.2.3　Coordination & subordination　/ 28

■ Unit 3　Developing a Logical Paragraph　/ 32

1. What is a paragraph?　/ 32
   1.1　Introduction　/ 32
   1.2　A logically ordered paragraph structure　/ 32
   1.3　Reading activity　/ 34
2. How do we develop a logical paragraph?　/ 36
   2.1　Controlling the topic　/ 36
   2.2　Unifying a paragraph　/ 37
   2.3　Connecting the sentences logically　/ 39
    2.3.1　Thematic progression (TP)—the smooth "flow" between sentences　/ 39
    2.3.2　The other cohesive devices—logical connectors　/ 43

■ Unit 4　Introducing the Research Topic　/ 47

1. What is the introduction to a research paper?　/ 47
   1.1　Introduction　/ 47
   1.2　The structural layout of an introduction　/ 47
   1.3　Reading activity　/ 48
2. How do we write the introduction section?　/ 52
   2.1　Establishing a research context/background　/ 52
   2.2　Writing a literature review　/ 55
    2.2.1　Previous studies　/ 55
    2.2.2　Research problems　/ 57
   2.3　Determining the purpose of the research　/ 59

2.4 Forming the outline of the paper / 60

Unit 5 Describing Research Methods / 63
1. What are the research methods? / 63
   1.1 Introduction / 63
   1.2 Structure of methods section / 63
   1.3 Reading activity / 64
2. How do we write the methods section? / 67
   2.1 Presenting experimental designs / 67
   2.2 Describing methods / 70
   2.3 Describing the experimental sampling method / 72
   2.4 Describing research materials or instruments / 76
   2.5 Narrating or explaining the experimental procedure / 79
   2.6 Collecting and analyzing the data / 82

Unit 6 Presenting Results and Discussing Major Findings / 85
1. What are the research results & discussion? / 85
   1.1 Introduction / 85
   1.2 Moves in writing R&D section / 86
   1.3 Reading activity / 86
2. How do we present research results and discuss the major findings? / 88
   2.1 Presenting research results / 88
   2.2 Discussing major findings / 93
   2.3 Using hedging words / 99

Unit 7 Writing an English Abstract / 104
1. What is the research paper abstract? / 104
   1.1 Introduction / 104

  1.2 The general format of an abstract / 105
    1.2.1 Types of abstracts / 105
    1.2.2 Structure of an abstract / 105
  1.3 Reading activity / 106
2. How do we write an English abstract? / 109
  2.1 Introducing the research topic / 109
  2.2 Presenting the used methods / 112
  2.3 Stating the results of the study / 115
  2.4 Making discussion or drawing conclusions / 116

Keys to Exercises / 120

Bibliography / 152

UNIT 1

Writing Academically

1. What is academic writing?

◆ 1.1 Introduction

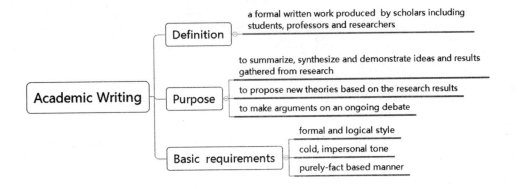

1.2 A well-structured academic research paper

An academic paper should be clearly and logically structured. The following is the basic structure of academic paper writing:

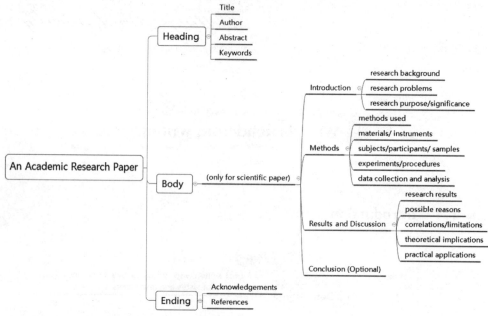

1.3 Reading activity

Task 1 Read a paper of your field and write the outline of the paper.

2. How do we write academically?

2.1 Using academic words

In academic writing, common English words tend to be replaced by academic words having more specific meanings.

Compare the words in the following table.

Parts of speech	Common words	Academic words
verbs	do	perform, implement, execute, complete, conduct, function, operate
	get	acquire, procure, receive, obtain, gain, achieve, attain
	give	provide, offer, supply, transfer, yield, allow, permit, enable, contribute
	go	proceed, pass, process, transfer, transmit
	find	determine, define, attain, locate, identify
	affect	influence, shape
	realize	comprehend, perceive, understand
	try	attempt, aim, aspire
	check	verify, confirm
	change	modify, adjust, alter, vary
	solve	alleviate, modify, resolve, eliminate, eradicate
	meet	satisfy, fulfill, adhere to
	consider	evaluate, assess
nouns	way	method, means, approach, strategy
	problem	limitation, restriction, obstacle, hindrance

(To be continued)

Parts of speech	Common words	Academic words
adjectives	different	distinct, diverse, various, varied
	little/few	seldom, slightly
	complicate	complex, cumbersome, intricate
	important	critical, crucial, essential, pertinent, relevant, significant, vital
	suitable	appropriate, adequate
adverbs	much/strongly	markedly, considerably, substantially
	very	highly, rather, quite, extremely

Task 2 Read the following sentences and replace the underlined words with academic words.

1. The study by Bussey & Bandura (1999) did (   ) the analysis of the gender role development from the perspective of social cognitive theory.
2. The findings of the studies prepared the ground for modern difference (   ) between the concepts of gender and sex.
3. Gender identity was viewed as the result of psychological development and thus it was viewed as a psychological problem (   ).
4. Psychoanalysis theory had a(n) important (   ) impact on the study of gender roles; however, there was lack of empirical research that led to various reformulations of the notion "gender" and approaches to its analysis.
5. Over decades, women tended to be more involved with private worries (   ) and relationships and the welfare of their own families.

Task 3 Turn the following common words into more academic ones.

help	
improve	
usually	
suitable	
whole	

Task 4 Find the appropriate academic words for the following phrases.

1. carry out
2. get rid of
3. look at carefully
4. look into
5. find out
6. a lot of
7. make sure
8. be made up of
9. make clear

◈ 2.2 Using nominalization

Nominalization is the expression of actions as noun phrases instead of verbs. By using nominalization, the academic paper may sound more abstract and objective. For example, we often use "judgment" rather than "judge" in academic writing.

Compare the following two sentences:

This information enables us to formulate precise questions.

This information enables the formulation of precise questions.

The second one is more academic and formal by changing the verb "to formulate" into the noun "formulation".

Task 5 Read the following sentences and underline the nominalized words.

1. Upon substitution of the actual magnitudes, v turned out to be the velocity of light.
2. All airfields in the country would be nationalized, and the government would continue with the development of new aircraft as recommended by the Brabazon Committee.
3. This is reflected in our admiration for people who have made something of their lives, sometimes against great odds, and in our somewhat disappointed judgment of those who merely drift through life.

4. Researchers have to judge the validity and reliability of the web sites.
5. The possibility of increasing dollar receipts was coupled with a belief that Africa could be a strategic centre for British power.
6. Depending on how unique (or unorthodox) the new method is, its validation probably should be established in a separate publication, published prior to submission of the main study.

Task 6 Turn the following words into nominalized words.

discover	
impair	
allow	
refuse	
propose	
indicate	
remove	
assume	
intend	
liable	
negligent	
extensive	
legal	
careless	
proficient	

2.3 Writing formally

Since academic writing is relatively formal, informality should be avoided. The following are some ways to avoid colloquial expressions.

a. Avoid using colloquial expressions, such as "stuff", "a lot of", "thing", "sort of".

b. Avoid using abbreviated forms, such as "can't", "doesn't", "shouldn't", "there's", "it's", and "won't".

c. Avoid using two-or-three-word verb phrases, such as "go on", "put up".

Task 7 Compare the following two texts and pay attention to their differences.

Academic	Non-academic
High temperature materials are necessary for the design of primary heat shields for future reusable space vehicles re-entering atmospheric planet at hypersonic velocity. During the reentry phase on earth, one of the most important phenomena occurring on the heat shield is the recombination of atomic oxygen and this phenomenon is more or less catalyzed by the material of the heat shield. (Balat-Pichelin & E. Bêche, 2010, p.4914)	When parents make a lot of rules about their children's behavior, they make trouble for themselves. I used to spend half my time making sure my rules were obeyed, and the other half answering questions like "Jack can get up whenever he likes, so why can't I?" or "Why can't I play with Angela? Jack's mum doesn't mind who he plays with." Or "Jack can drink anything he likes. Why can't I drink wine too?"

2.4 Writing concisely

Conciseness means to write what needs to be written in as few words as possible while essential information should not be sacrificed. The words or phrases chosen for academic writing should be the most effective ones.

Compare the following two sentences in the table.

Wordy	Concise
The positive control exhibited an increase of 14%, the negative control exhibited an increase of 3%, and the experimental group exhibited an increase of 16%.	The positive control exhibited an increase of 14%; the negative control an increase of 3%, and the experimental group an increase of 16%.
In logistics, simple transaction data and averaging are often used to allocate direct costs.	Logistics often uses simple transaction data and averaging to allocate direct costs.

Task 8 Improve the following sentences into more concise ones.

1. The tissue was minced and the samples were incubated.
2. As a result of these experiments it became quite evident overheating of the samples had occurred.
3. It was suggested by Dr. Smith that the test be postponed.
4. The installation of the new equipment has been carried out.
5. Our preliminary report included a description of the techniques used for the infusion of fluids into the cerebral ventricles of rats.

2.5　Avoiding plagiarism

Plagiarism is the improper use of others' ideas, words or methods without clearly acknowledging the source of that information. If you use another person's material, you must acknowledge your source. Thus, to avoid plagiarism, a writer should learn how to use citations properly.

APA citations style, commonly used for academic paper, refers to the rules and conventions established by the American Psychological Association for documenting sources. APA style requires both in-text citations and a reference list. For every in-text citation there should be a full citation in the reference list and vice versa.

2.5.1　APA in-text citations—direct (quotations) and indirect citations

An APA in-text citation includes only three items: the last name(s) of the author(s), the year the source was published, and sometimes the page or location of the information.

a. Quotations

A quotation must be identical to the original, accurate in every sense including the punctuation, and must be put between quotation marks. They must match the source document word for word and must be attributed to the original author.

The following are some basic sentence structures for shorter quotations.

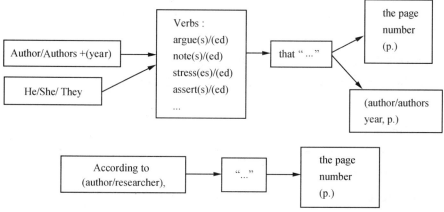

Read the following samples:

- Byrne and Trew (2005) argue, "To be effective, interventions that aim to reduce or prevent offending behaviour need to be based on a sound understanding of what leads people to offend, and what leads people to stop offending" (185).
- "Whatever his decision, he would have to take account of his own strong feelings about cheating the effect on career, and the effect on other students' morale" (Shapira, 1993, p.31).
- Hayes (2000) states that proto-themes represent the beginning of a theme and "will develop and change as the analysis proceeds" (176).
- Interpreting these results, Robbins et al. (2003) suggested that the "therapists in dropout cases may have inadvertently validated parental negativity about the adolescent without adequately responding to the adolescent's needs or concerns" (p.541), contributing to an overall climate of negativity.

If the direct quotation is longer than 40 words, omit the quotation marks and start the quotation on a new line, indented five spaces from the left margin. See the following samples:

• Sample 1:

Grabe and Kaplan (1996) state as follows:

L1 students have some implicit knowledge of rhetorical plans, organizational logic, and genre form in their native language; it is not at all clear that students have the same implicit knowledge with respect to L2 (p.142).

• Sample 2:

She further insisted that inexperienced ESL writers need "rhetorical acculturation" by saying as follows:

Inexperienced and unskilled ESL writers who have not been exposed to rhetorical analyses of American academic prose need to develop their understanding of the forms of academic prose, and they need to have the opportunity to practice those formats …[because] their approaches to rhetorical forms differ from the approach of native speakers (Reid, 1984, p.151).

Task 9 **Write quotations according to the information given below.**

■ The original sentence

Dancers love to suffer, and while they wallow in tragedy, they alienate and bore their audiences.

Last name of the author/researcher: Humphrey

Year/time: (1959)

Page number: P.40

■ The original sentence

The main purpose of a dictionary is to prevent or at last reduce communication conflicts which may arise from lexical deficit.

Last name of the author/researcher: Hartmann

Year/time: (1987)

Page number: p.21

■ The original sentence

Students often had difficulty using APA style, especially when it was their first time.

Last name of the author/researcher: Jones

Year/time: 1998

Page number: 100

■ The original sentences

Students often had difficulty using APA style, especially when it was their first time citing sources. This difficulty could be attributed to the fact that many students failed to purchase a style manual or to ask their teacher for help.

Last name of the author/researcher: Jones

Year/time: 1998

Page number: 100

b. Indirect citations

Usually there are two forms of in-text citations: a narrative in-text citation and a parenthetical citation.

For example,

> 1. Stein (2018) studied whether the early onset of Alzheimer's disease affected individual younger than 30. (p. 42)
> 2. Another study found similar data, showing that individuals as young as 18 displayed symptoms of the disease. (Tang & Pierce, 2014, p. 231)

In a narrative in-text citation, the author's name is in the text of the sentence and the page number is at the end of the sentence as Example 1. Example 2 is parenthetical citation. In parentheses are the names of the authors, year published and page number.

The following is the common format of APA in-text citation.

Authors and sources	Format	Examples
A work by one author or two authors	Last name, year Last name A & last name B, year	Stahl (1983) Stoleman and O'Connor (1986)
A work by three to five authors	Last name, last name, and last name, year	Taatgen, Van Rijn, and Anderson (2007)
Six or more authors	Last name A et al., year	(Taatgen et al., 2007)
Authors with the same last name	Initials. last name, year	(R. Ellis, 2002) (N. Ellis, 2002)
Two or more works by the same author	Last name, year, year or last name, the same year a, the same year b	(Zhang, 1997) (Zhang, 1999) (Zhang, 2004) (Zhang, 1997, 1999, 2004) (Bloom, 2003a, 2003b)
Two or more works in the same parenthesis	Last name, year; last name, year	(Brown, 2001; Sullivan, Weinert & Fulton, 1993; Weinert & Burman, 1994)
Unknown authors	Title of the entry, year or Anonymous, year	(Sleep Medicine, 2001) (anonymous, 2002)
Organization as an author	Name of the organization, year	(Columbia University, 1987, p.54)
Classical works	Last name, tran. year or Last name, original year of publication / latest year of publication	(Caldwell, trans. 1954) (Bat, 1900/1943)
Indirect/secondary sources	As cited in last name, year	(as cited in Myers, 2003, p.57)
Electronic source with author and date	The same format as a published work	(Henry, 2009)
Electronic source with no author and no date	Put the title or a part of the title in quotation mark, then abbreviation n.d. for "no date"	"College Students and Study Habits", n.d.
Sources without page numbers	Last name, year, para (the abbreviation of a paragraph)	(Hall, 2001, para.5)

(To be continued)

Authors and sources	Format	Examples
Personal communications (private letters, memos, personal interviews, and electronic communications)	Last name, personal communication, Date	George, personal communication, June 8, 1985

Task 10 Write in-text citations with the information given below.

1. (Jones), (APA style is a difficult citation format for first-time learners.), (1998)
2. (Breen and Maassen), (conducted a two-phase research project, that firstly explored student perceptions of plagiarism and then developed learning materials to be embedded within courses.), (2005)
3. (Stoleman and O'Connor), (argue that it is better for a writer to discuss a narrow aspect of a large topic in detail than to attempt to discuss loose generalizations), (1986), (p.4).
4. (Barker et al.), (investigated the difficulties faced by visited Asian students at Australian universities and suggest that schemes that help to provide friendship and informal skills training will be beneficial to the newly arrived student), (1991)
5. (Furnham and Bochner), (It has been suggested by), (that practical culture learning experiences can relieve some of the distress experienced by individuals adapting to a new cultural environment), (1986)
6. (O'Malley & Valdez Pierce), (Genesee & Upshur), (in many disciplines, portions and learning by providing portraits of students, offering multidimensional perspectives, encouraging students to participate, and linking teaching), (1996), (1996)

2.5.2 APA reference style

Apart from in-text citations, reference list should be written at the end of a paper. The reference list, often entitled as "References", is an alphabetical list of works cited, or works to which you have made reference. Read the following samples.

- **Sample 1**

Rossi, P. H. (1989). *Down and Out in America: The Origins of Homelessness.* Chicago: University of Chicago Press.

| Last name, Initials. | (Year). | Title of the work. (in italics) | Place of publication: | Publishing company. |

- **Sample 2**

| Last name, initials., | (Year). | Title of the article. |

O'Brien, D., Slack, T. (2003). An analysis of change in an organizational field: The professionalization of English Rugby Union. *Journal of Sport Management,* 17(4), 417–448.

| Name of the journal (in italics). | Journal volume number | (Journal issue number), | Page range across which the article occurs. (do not use "p." or "pp.") |

The following are the guidelines for an APA style reference list.

a. Variations on the book reference format

Author(s)	Reference list (examples)
One author; Two authors; Three or more authors (list all authors)	① Baddeley, A. D. (1999). *Essentials of Human Memory.* Hove, England: Psychology Press. ② Beck, C. A. J. & Sales, B. D. (2001). *Family Mediation: Facts, Myths, and Future Prospects.* Washington, DC: American Psychological Association. ③ Booth, W. C., Colomb, G. B. & Williams, J. M. (1995). *The Craft of Research.* Chicago: University of Chicago Press.
Book with editor(s) and no author	Zhang, W. Y. (Ed.) (2003). *Global Perspectives: Philosophy and Practice in Distance Education.* Beijing: China Central Radio & Television University Press.

(To be continued)

Author(s)	Reference list(examples)
Article or chapter in an edited book	Duckworth, J. C. & Levitt, E. E. (1994). Minnesota Multiphasic Personality Inventory-2. In D. J. Keyser & R. C. Sweetland (Eds.), *Test Critiques*: Vol. 10 (pp. 424-428). Austin, TX: Pro-Ed.
Organization	American Psychiatric Association. (1994). *Diagnostic and Statistical Manual of Mental Disorders* (4th ed.). Washington, DC: Author.

b. Variations on the journal reference format

Author(s)	Reference list (examples)
One to six authors Or (list all)	① Kember, D. (2001). Orientations to enrolment of part-time students: A classification system based upon students' perceived lifelong learning. *Higher Education Research & Development*, 20(3), 265-280. ② Klimoski, R. & Palmer, S. (1993). The ADA and the hiring process in organizations. *Consulting Psychology Journal: Practice and Research*, 45(2), 10-36. ③ Saywi Kernis, M. H., Cornell, D. P., Sun, C. R., Berry, A. & Harlow, T. (1993). There's more to self-esteem than whether it is high or low: The importance of stability of self-esteem. *Journal of Personality and Social Psychology*, 65(6), 1190-1204.
More than seven authors (include the first six, then insert an ellipsis (…) and the last name)	Miller, F. H., Choi, M. J., Angeli, L. L., Harland, A. A., Stamos, J. A., Thomas, S. T., … Rubin, L. H. (2009). Web site usability for the blind and low-vision user. *Technical Communication*, 57, 323-335.
Unpublished manuscript	Borst, W. U. (1996). *Guidelines for Writing in APA Style*. Unpublished manuscript, Troy State University at Phenix City.

c. Reference format of electronic media

Electronic source	Reference list (examples)
Online books or articles	① VandenBos, G., Knapp, S. & Doe, J. (2001). Role of reference elements in the selection of resources by psychology undergraduates [Electronic version]. *Journal of Bibliographic Research*, 5, 117–123. ② Hodges, F. M. (2003). The promised planet: Alliances and struggles of the gerontocracy in American television science fiction of the 1960s. *The Aging Male*, 6, 175–182. Retrieved from http://www.informaworld.com/TheAgingMale. ③ Star trek planet classifications. (n. d.). In *Wikipedia*. Retrieved January 7, 2009, from http://en.wikipedia.org/wiki/Star_Trek_planet_classifications.
Articles from one's blog	Zompist. (2009, September 30). Star wars: Hope not so new anymore [Web log message]. Retrieved from http://zompist.wordpress.com/2009/09/30/star-wars-hope-not-so-new-anymore/.
Videos	Crusade2267. (2006, November 02). For the uniform: One fan's obsession with Star trek, part 1 [Video file]. Retrieved from http://www.youtube.com/watch? v=ul5q4PTME-M.
PowerPoint slides	Oard, D. W. (2001). Bringing Star trek to life: Computers that speak and listen [PowerPoint slides]. Retrieved from University of Maryland TerpConnect website: http://terpconnect.umd.edu/~oard/papers/cpsp118t.ppt.

Task 11 Make corrections to the following reference list.

Works cited

Balagura, Steve. (1968). "Influence of Osmotic and Caloric Loads Upon Lateral Hypothalamic Self-Stimulation" Journal of Comparative and Physiological Psychology, 66, 325–328.

Abel, S. E., Fox, P. T., Potley, J. R. (1997). Insights from recent positron emission tomographic studies of drug abuse and dependence. Current Opinion in Psychiatry, 19(3), 246–252.

Abel, S. E., Fox, P. T., Posner, J. P. (1998). Positron emission tomographic studies of the cortical anatomy of single word processing. Nature, 331, pp.585 –589.

Codon, D.E. (1994, January 10). Kids growing up scared. Newsweek, volume 73, issue 3, pp.43 –49.

Klatzky, R. L. (1980). Human Memory: Structures and Processes (Second Edition). Friedman: San Francisco, CA.

Swaminathan, N. (2007). Eating Disorders. Psychology today website Psychologytoday.com. Found on 11/13/07.

UNIT 2

Forming an Effective Academic Sentence

1. What is a sentence?

◆ 1.1 Introduction

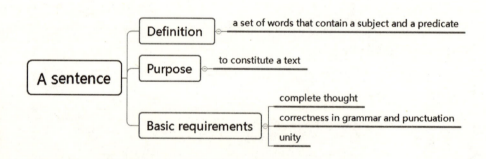

◆ 1.2 A tree-like English sentence

An English sentence is like a tree because its basic patterns can be expanded by adding words, phrases, or clauses as modifiers as they tend to develop in the way as a big tree grows with its branches produced from their stems. Read the following samples.

Unit 2　Forming an Effective Academic Sentence

- Sample 1

　　The discovery that Haydn's and Mozart's symphonies were conducted during their lifetimes by a pianist who played the chords to keep the orchestra together has given rise to early music recordings in which a piano can be heard obtrusively in the foreground.

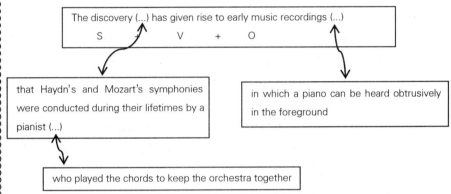

　　Sample 1 is a complex sentence with three clauses. The underlined parts form a main clause structure.

- Sample 2

　　Moreover, concerning task performance and further attesting to divergent validity, the lack of perseverance was the only aspect of impulsivity to show a significant positive correlation with proactive interference index based on errors.

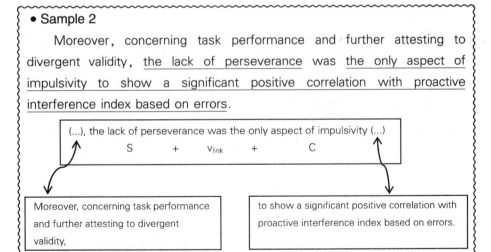

　　The above sample is a simple sentence structure ($S + V_{link}$). It looks very complicated because it has complex noun phrases (NPs). Pay attention to the underlined parts in the above sentence.

1.3 Reading activity

Task 1 Read the following sentences and draw sentence trees as Sample 1 and 2.

1. Although our data provide more information concerning the processes related to urgency and lack of perseverance, the absence of relations with the other two dimensions may also help to extend preliminary support for a model of the separate cognitive processes involved in the four facets of impulsivity.
2. The investigation of mental intrusions in relation to inhibition and impulsivity should benefit from finer-grained distinctions between different kinds of interfering thoughts in different tasks or activities.
3. In other words, individuals who experience more urgency and have more pronounced difficulties with prepotent response inhibition showed diminished effects of proactive interference, as reflected by the log of the reaction times.
4. The monkey projects demonstrate that, compared with control animals that eat normally, caloric-restricted monkeys have lower body temperatures and levels of the pancreatic hormone insulin, and they retain more youthful levels of certain hormones that tend to fall with age.
5. The rat findings have been replicated many times and extended to creatures ranging from yeast to fruit flies, worms, fish, spiders, mice and hamsters.

Task 2 Complete the following sentences by translating the Chinese in the brackets into English.

1. Validity refers to _____(实验结果的信度) and the degree to which the results can be applied to the general population of interest.

2. The complexity of scientific inquiry necessitates that _____ _____(方法部分的写作要清晰有序,避免混淆和模糊).
3. It is worth noting that _____(引入任何测量变量的新方法), or preparing/designing a model will require intense discussion.
4. The methods section is the most important part of a research paper because _____(它提供了读者判断研究有效性所需要的信息).
5. Compound sentence structures should be avoided, _____ _____(以及描述不重要的细节).
6. A study design is simply a strategy to control and manipulate variables that _____(为……研究问题提供了答案) regarding potential cause-and-effect relationships.
7. The rationale and assumptions on which experimental procedures are based should be briefly stated in the methods section and, _____ _____(必要时在讨论一节中更详细地说明).
8. The internal validity of a study is judged by _____ (其结果在多大程度上可归因于) manipulation of independent variables and not to the effects of confounding variables.
9. Although many clustering algorithms have been proposed, it is very difficult _____(找到适合各类数据集的聚类方法).
10. Data clustering refers to finding similar objects within groups or clusters where the objects of a cluster have the highest similarities with one another but they _____(与其他群组内的对象不同).

Task 3 Translate the following sentences into English.
1. 大多数公司和人才市场所需要的不是机器人,而是能够提出想法的创造性人才。
2. 在精神层面,如果孩子花费太多时间在虚拟世界中生活,他们可能失去以正常的方式交友和社交的能力。

3. 毫无疑问,政府必须制定环保政策,并尽其所能实现变革,但我们个人也可以发挥至关重要的作用。

2. How do we form an effective academic sentence?

▶ 2.1　Expanding sentences with noun phrases (NPs)

Most sentences follow the seven basic patterns. Look at the following table.

	Basic sentence patterns	Examples
1	S+V (subject+predicative verb)	John has gone out to buy some books.
2	S+V (link verb) +C (complement)	This new invention will prove useful to all humanity.
3	S+V+O (object)	We can reach the city in half an hour.
4	S+V+o+O	He has rendered me great help in time of need.
5	S+V+O+C	He painted the house green.
6	"It"…	It is important for us to learn English.
7	"There be"…	There is a ball under the table.

English academic sentences are expanded ones based on their basic patterns since long sentences are often considered specific to explain complicated ideas clearly and precisely. Therefore, complicated noun phrases (NPs) which function grammatically as nouns within sentences as the subject or object of a verb are used.

Most NPs have a noun as their head with the pre-modifiers and post-modifiers. Pre-modifiers are words that modify or describe nouns and that occur before the noun. They consist of determiners, pronouns, adjectives, participles (both -ed and -ing) and nouns or noun adjuncts. A post-modifier or complement may be a prepositional phrase, a relative clause, certain adjective or participial phrases, or a dependent clause or infinitive phrase appropriate to the noun.

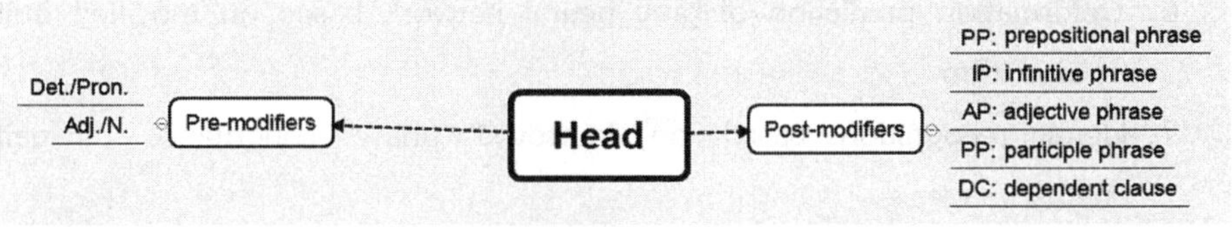

Look at the following examples:

A noun phrase			
Pre-modifiers		Head	Post-modifiers
the	tall	man	in the yard
an	attractive young college	student	to whom you were talking
his	black	coat	made in Japan

Read the following sentence and pay attention to the noun phrases.

> Research done in this area has led to sophisticated techniques with reduced computation time and improved the capability of systems to address the intricate problem offered in stock markets to trend prediction.

In the above sentence, the underlined parts are noun phrases which serve as subject and object of the sentence. The headword "research" is the subject, while the headwords "techniques" and "capability" serve as objects in the sentence.

Task 4 The following are English titles of some research papers. Identify the headword of each NP and translate them into Chinese.

1. A Collaborative Filtering Recommendation Algorithm Based on Item Rating Prediction
2. Self-localization systems and algorithms for wireless sensor networks
3. Multiple faults fuzzy diagnosis for complicated system based on grey theory
4. Detection probability calculation and performance evaluation of single pulse

radar

5. Database design of information quality inspection system for geoinformation products
6. Deformation prediction of grey neural network based on modified fruit fly algorithm
7. Identity recognition based on improved phase congruency of gait energy image
8. Polymorphic ant colony clamping planning based on the machining operation unit
9. An optimized deep learning algorithm of convolutional neural network
10. Wavelet entropy denoising algorithm of electrocadiogram signals based on correlation
11. Reinforcement learning algorithm for path following control of articulated vehicle
12. Multi-objective optimization of hybrid electrical vehicle based on immune genetic algorithm

Task 5 Translate the following phrases into English.

1. 公共关系的焦点
2. 环境问题比如温室气体的排放
3. 失业率的上升
4. 农村缺少基础建设和政府资助
5. 对儿童的心算产生不利影响

Task 6 Read the following sentences and underline the NPs and circle the headword in each NPs.

1. Women's immune response to allergens weakens with each successive pregnancy.
2. A good source of information which can be found on the Internet is the online journal *Science Direct*.
3. Thus, the tasks used in this study to evaluate prepotent response inhibition

and resistance to proactive interference may be of primary interest for the laboratory assessment of cognitive aspects related to distinct facets of impulsivity, namely urgency and the lack of perseverance, respectively.
4. The dissociation of inhibitory function related to urgency and the lack of perseverance may shed some light on certain processes involved in some psychopathological conditions.
5. As for sensation seeking, the absence of any relationship with inhibition in this study or with decision-making processes, as shown in a previous one (Zermatten et al., 2005), may underscore the fact that this facet of impulsivity is not related to executive control.
6. It is noteworthy that as predicted in our hypothesis, the lack of premeditation and sensation seeking were found to be unrelated to inhibition performances, which indicates that these two dimensions may depend on other psychological processes.
7. The average distance travelled to their "main" store by the 276 respondents who switched to the new store, fell by 2.25 kms in the pre-intervention period to 0.98 kms in the post-intervention period.
8. Judging the external validity of a study involving human subjects requires that descriptive data be provided regarding the basic demographic profile of the sample population, including age, gender, and possibly the racial composition of the sample.
9. Theory and research in psychology show that a thorough understanding of an individual's view of an issue or problem is an essential requirement for successful change of that person's attitudes and behaviour.
10. University policy on academic integrity/misconduct defines the behaviours that all stakeholders must abide by, and the parameters for reporting, investigating and penalising infringements.

2.2 Writing correct sentences

2.2.1 Subject-verb agreements

The subject-verb agreement means that a subject and its predicative verb match in form. For example, a third-person singular subject takes a predicative verb with -s if the verb is in the present tense.

• Sample 1

The explosion in demand for accommodation in the inner suburbs of Melbourne suggests a recent change in many people's preferences as to where they live.

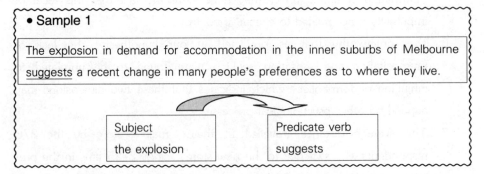

Subject	Predicate verb
the explosion	suggests

The subject in this sentence "the explosion" and the predicate verb "suggests" must match in number and in person.

• Sample 2

Either the samples or the apparatus was contaminated.

Task 7 Fill in the blanks with the proper verb forms.

1. These data _____ (to be) significant.
2. Statistics _____ (to show) that a teacher shortage is coming.
3. K-means _____ (to be) one of the popular and fast clustering algorithms.
4. The rest of the paper _____ (to be) organized as follows.
5. Of course, there _____ (to be) some skeptics who doubt the self-

esteem movement's claim to address widespread social problems.
6. For those with high achievement needs, typically a minority in any organization, the existence of external goals _____ (to be) less important because high achievers are already internally motivated.
7. In Canfield's seminars, either his team leaders or Canfield himself _____ (to ask) participants to make up events, act out their responses, and explain the outcomes.
8. Some of the more obvious rewards that managers allocate _____ (to include) pay, promotions, autonomy, job scope and depth, and the opportunity to participate in goal-setting and decision-making.
9. Swarm Intelligence algorithms, the algorithms based on population behavior and self-organization of social insects and animals, _____ (to be considered) as an evolving alternatives to KHM clustering algorithm.
10. In addition, this paper presents several modern algorithms for multi-objective optimization, which _____ (be not applied) to this problem domain previously.

2.2.2 Pronoun-antecedent agreements

The pronoun-antecedent agreement means that pronouns must match the form of their antecedent.

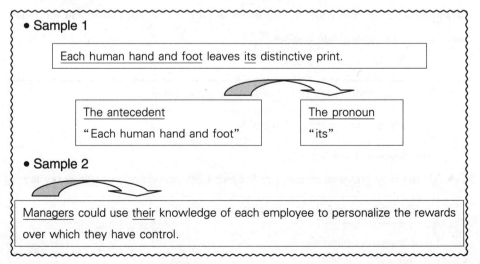

Task 8 Fill in the blanks with proper pronouns.

1. Unlike other cereals, corn bears little resemblance to _____ ancestors.
2. Many people wonder what gives certain leaders _____ spark and magnetic personal appeal.
3. The suburb he inhabits has no essential vitality of _____ own and is a mere roost where he comes at day's end to go to sleep.
4. Usually, it is not the quiet, low-profile manager but rather the charismatic manager with strong leadership qualities who convinces others that _____ best interests are served by the course of action _____ will be proposing.
5. Unfortunately, for maximum benefit, people would probably have to reduce _____ caloric intake by roughly thirty per cent, equivalent to dropping from 2,500 calories a day to 1,750.

2.2.3 Coordination & subordination

Both coordination and subordination involve the linking of units of the same rank. The major difference is that coordination links the ideas that are equal in importance while subordination links the ideas that are unequal in weight. Through subordination, the major idea is expressed in an independent clause and the minor idea(s) are in subordinate clauses.

Read the following examples.

- The young man is honest, hardworking and reliable.

  | honest ‖ hardworking ‖ reliable |

  (coordination of words)

- TV not only brings us amusement but also plays an educational role in our life.

  | brings us amusement ‖ plays an educational role in our life |

  (coordination of phrases)

Unit 2 Forming an Effective Academic Sentence

- Findings indicate <u>that only half of the participants had read the policy on plagiarism</u> and <u>that confusion regarding what behaviour constitutes plagiarism was evident</u>.

  | that only half of the participants had read the policy on plagiarism ‖ that confusion regarding what behaviour constitutes plagiarism was evident |

  (coordination of clauses)

- Essentially, <u>each patient is represented by a feature vector</u>, <u>which serves as the input to the similarity measure</u>.

  | each patient is represented by a feature vector | (main clause)

  | which serves as the input to the similarity measure |

  (subordinate clause)

- More specifically, <u>if two patients have the same label information</u>, <u>it means that they are considered similar</u>.

  | it means that they are considered similar |

  (main clause)

  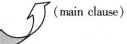

  | if two patients have the same label information |

  (subordinate clause)

Task 9 Read the following sentences and underline the coordinate or subordinate construction of each sentence.

1. Finally, a possible framework for understanding the impacts of tourism on health and their interrelationships has been identified.
2. Scientists have studied poison ivy infection for centuries, but they have found no preventive pills or inoculation.
3. On the other hand, some cohorts do not represent the entire patient distribution, which often leads to bad base metric.
4. Given these two definitions, both homogeneous and heterogeneous neighborhoods are constructed for all patients in the training data.
5. In particular, the homogeneous neighborhood of the index patient is the set of retrieved patients that are close in distance measure to the index patient and are also considered similar by the physician.
6. It will never be known how and when this numeration ability developed, but it is certain that numeration was well developed by the time humans had formed even semi-permanent settlements.
7. We formulate the problem as a supervised metric learning problem, where physician input is used as the supervision information.
8. Finally, we demonstrated the use cases through a clinical decision support prototype and quantitatively compared the proposed methods against baselines, where significant performance gain is obtained.
9. We construct features from longitudinal sequences of observable measures based on demographics, medication, lab, vital signs and symptoms.
10. The second and the third techniques address other related challenges of using such a supervised metric, namely how to update the learned similar metric with new evidence efficiently and how to combine multiple physicians' opinions.

Unit 2 Forming an Effective Academic Sentence

Task 10 Read the following sentences and fill in the blanks with proper conjunctions.

1. The goal is to learn the similarity that pushes patients of the same diagnosis closer, _____ patient of different diagnosis far away from each other.
2. Obtaining high quality training data is very important _____ often challenging, since it typically imposes overhead on users, who are busy physicians in our case.
3. We formulate this problem as a quadratic optimization problem _____ propose an efficient alternating strategy to find the optimal solution.
4. In this section, we present a prototype system _____ uses patient similarity for clinical decision support.
5. The idea is that because some cohorts represent well the entire patient distribution, _____ often leads to good base metric.
6. Two questionnaires were developed for the survey, _____ were translated into Chinese and modified according to the feedback from 10 respondents.
7. Nowadays, the emergency of new infectious diseases _____ the reemergence of diseases are causing concern, and travel is a major contributor to their spread.
8. From the figures we can see that Comdi significantly outperforms other secure version methods _____ can achieve almost the same performance as the shared version of LSML.
9. Different types of clinical events arise in different frequency _____ in different orders.
10. In this section, we present a supervised metric learning algorithm _____ can incorporate physician feedback as supervision information.

UNIT 3

Developing a Logical Paragraph

1. What is a paragraph?

◆ 1.1 Introduction

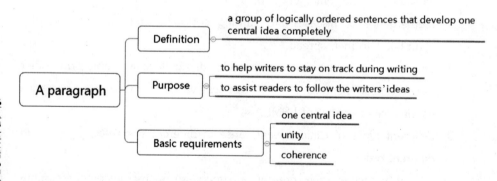

◆ 1.2 A logically ordered paragraph structure

Different paragraphs have different functions. Some paragraphs introduce, conclude, or provide transitions. Most paragraphs, however, are topical paragraphs, which consist of a statement of a main idea and specific, logical

Unit 3 Developing a Logical Paragraph

support for that main idea.

Thus, paragraphs usually have two important components—a topic sentence and supporting sentences.

For example,

> ① Jack shouldn't have taken the gymnastics course. ② In September, he fell off the uneven bars and got a concussion. ③ A month later he sprained his ankle, after a bad landing off the balance beam. ④ In January, he broke his thumb when he caught it on the bar of the pommel horse. ⑤ He also broke the support beam in the basement of his parent's home, showing them his skills when he was home for the December holidays. ⑥ His academic luck was no better than his physical luck: he failed the mid-semester exam in November and the final exam in January in his gymnastics course. ⑦ The result of his bad luck was that he failed to graduate in May, due to the lack of two hours of physical education credit. (杨俊峰, 2003, p.125)
>
> ```
>                    topic sentence ①
>        ┌──────┬──────┬──────┬──────┐
>   supporting supporting supporting supporting supporting
>   sentence ② sentence ③ sentence ④ sentence ⑤ sentence ⑥
>        └──────┴──────┴──────┴──────┘
>               concluding sentence ⑦
> ```

In the above paragraph, the first sentence is the topic sentence which contains the main idea of the paragraph. Others back up and explain the main idea. They explain the topic sentence by giving evidence. And all the sentences in the paragraph are closely related and well connected.

1.3 Reading activity

Task 1 Find out the topic sentence, supporting sentences and concluding sentence (if there is any) of each paragraph.

1. ① Hurricanes, which are also called cyclones, exert tremendous power. ② These violent storms are often a hundred miles in diameter, and their winds can reach velocities of seventy-five miles per hour or more. ③ Furthermore, the strong winds and heavy rainfall that accompany them can completely destroy a small town in a couple of hours. ④ The energy that is released by a hurricane in one day exceeds the total energy consumed by humankind throughout the world in one year.

2. ① Statistics on morality and hospital admissions show that death rates increase during extremely hot days, particularly among very old and very young people living in cities. ② In July 1995, a heat wave killed more than 700 people in the Chicago area alone. ③ Studies based on these types of statistics estimate that in Atlanta, for example, even a warming of about two degrees (F) would increase heat-related deaths from 78 today to anywhere from 96 to 247 people per year. ④ If people are able to install air conditioning and otherwise acclimatize themselves to the hotter temperatures, the lower estimate is more likely.

3. ① Many old buildings in cities are still being found useful. ② In several cities, old buildings that were no longer being used have been converted to a variety of useful structures. ③ For example, one school building was changed into ninety-nine rental units for elderly and low income residents. ④ In Baltimore, Maryland, six schools were converted into 132 units with the help of a four-million-dollar city bond financing arrangement. "School House 77" in Boston utilizes three recycled elementary schools and an abandoned instrument factory. ⑤ All these examples show how cities are using unneeded schools, police stations, libraries, and boarded-up factories that are structurally sound and even architecturally interesting buildings.

Unit 3 Developing a Logical Paragraph

4. ① The history of money is interesting. ② Bronze coins were probably invented in ancient China, but they were not round in shape. ③ The Lydians in 600 BC were the first to produce those. ④ They stamped special images and marks on the sides of the coins. ⑤ As time went on, trade among countries increased, and coins came into even wider use. ⑥ It is likely that the ancient Chinese also developed some form of paper money, but it was not until 1661 that a Swedish bank issued paper bank notes. ⑦ In 1988 Australia introduced durable, recyclable plastic bank notes.

Task 2 Read the following information about "Brain Size and Intelligence". Rearrange the sentences and write a paragraph with the information.

1. The possessor of this mammoth brain is an intelligent animal.
2. The largest dinosaurs weighed as much as 100 tons.
3. It is interesting to compare the brain of a very large dinosaur with the brain of an equally large modern mammal like the whale.
4. The brain of a large whale is a huge mass of grey matter, nearly a foot and a half across, that weighs about 20 pounds.
5. Yet that small amount of grey matter had to exercise control over the same 100-ton bulk that is commanded by the 20-pound brain of the largest whales.
6. Some whales have a remarkable memory capacity: they can memorize a complex whale song that goes on for hours, and repeat it note for note a year later.
7. Whales also weigh as much as 100 tons and are, as the dinosaurs were in their time, the largest animals alive today.
8. The brains of the largest dinosaurs, on the other hand, such as supersaurus, were only the size of an orange and weighed about half a pound.

2. How do we develop a logical paragraph?

A logical paragraph should have the following two basic elements: unity and coherence. A paragraph is unified if all the sentences in the paragraph lead to one central idea. What's more, the sentences in a paragraph should be arranged in a clear and logical order.

◆ 2.1 Controlling the topic

A topic sentence should always contain both a topic and a controlling idea. The controlling idea commits the paragraph to a specific aspect of the topic, and it advises the reader of the subject to be discussed and how the paragraph will discuss it.

Take the following paragraph as an example.

> All these islands are <u>very beautiful, and distinguished by various qualities</u>. They are accessible and full of a great variety of trees stretching up to the stars, the leaves of which I believe are never shed, for I saw them as green and flourishing as they are usually in Spain in the month of May. Some of them were blossoming, and some were bearing fruit, some were in other conditions. Each one was thriving in its own way. The nightingale and various other birds without number were singing, in the month of November, when I was exploring them.

The topic sentence of the above paragraph contains a controlling idea, which narrows down the topic. With the key words "beautiful", "distinguished", and the phrase "various qualities", the central idea will be easily developed.

Unit 3 Developing a Logical Paragraph

Task 3 Read the following sentences and underline the controlling idea in each sentence.

1. Pollution has become a serious problem about which we worry.
2. Somatic cell enhancement engineering should not be performed because it would be morally precarious.
3. Some language loss, like species loss, is natural and predictable.
4. Repressive language policies are common in many parts of the world.
5. Synonyms, words that have the same basic meaning, do not always have the same emotional meaning.

2.2 Unifying a paragraph

Unity means one or more sentences focusing on a single idea or topic. If all the sentences in a paragraph lead to one central idea, then the paragraph is unified.

- Sample 1

① My father's face <u>is rough</u>. ② His complexion is leathery and wrinkled. ③ There are large pores in his skin that covers his nose and cheeks. ④ His nose, broken twice in his life, makes him look like a boxer who has lost too many fights. ⑤ His mouth, unless he smiles, looks hard and threatening. ⑥ His chin is massive and angular. Shaved or not, my father's face is rugged. (杨俊峰, 2003, p.138)

In the above paragraph, the topic sentence is "My father's face is rough." In order to support the central idea "rough", the writer carefully describes his father's complexion, nose, cheeks, mouth and chin. Therefore, the sentences ②, ③, ④, ⑤, ⑥ serve as supporting sentences.

• Sample 2

| ① Individuals in every culture have similar basic needs but express them differently. ② In daily life we all initiate conversation, use formal and informal speech, give praise, express disagreement, seek information, and extend invitations. ③ Some of the verbal patterns we use are influenced by our culture. ④ Whereas directness in speech is common in the United States, indirectness is the rule in parts of the Far East. ⑤ Thus people from both of these parts of the world would probably express criticism of others differently. | Sentence ①
Topic and its controlling idea

Sentences ② ③ ④
Supporting sentences

Sentence ⑤
Conclusion |

Task 4 Compare the following two paragraphs which discuss the same topic and choose the one that is unified.

1. (1) Progress is gradually being made in the fight against cancer. (2) In the early 1900s, few cancer patients had any hope of long-term survival. (3) In the 1930s, less than one in five cancer victims lived more than five years. (4) In the 1950s, the ratio was one in four, and in the 1960s, it was one three. (5) Currently, four of ten patients who get cancer this year will be alive five years from now. (6) The gain from one in four to four in ten represents about 69,000 lives saved each year.

2. (1) Progress is gradually being made in the fight against cancer. (2) In the early 1900s, few cancer patients had any hope of long-term survival. (3) But because of advances in medical technology, progress has been made so that currently four in ten cancer patients survive. (4) It has been proven that smoking is a direct cause of lung cancer. (5) However, that battle has not yet been won. (6) Although cures for some forms of cancer have been discovered, other forms of cancer are still increasing. (7) Heart disease is also increasing. (杨俊峰, 2003, p.137)

◈ 2.3 Connecting the sentences logically

Coherence refers to connection and organization. A coherent text is one in which the sentences are arranged in a clear, logical order, and the transitions are smooth and natural.

2.3.1 Thematic progression (TP)—the smooth "flow" between sentences

Thematic progression (TP pattern) consists of two parts, theme and rheme. "Theme in a clause is the element which serves as the point of departure of the message, it is that with which the clause is concerned, while rheme is the part of the clause in which the theme is developed" (Halliday, 1994, p. 37). In other words, the theme (T) is usually known (or given) information while the rheme (R) is new information. The T-R connection of various types is called "thematic progression".

For example,

> Last week I (T1) went to the theatre (R1). I (T2 =T1) had a very good seat (R2).
>
> T1 (I) ⟶ R1 (theatre)
> T2 (=T1)(I) ⟶ R2 (a good seat)

There are mainly five types of thematic progression often used in academic writing. They are simple linear pattern, constant pattern, concentrated pattern, derived pattern and crossing pattern. These TP patterns jointly appear and contribute to the development of a text.

Types of TP	Models
simple linear pattern	T1—R1 T2 (=R1)—R2 T3 (=R2)—R3 Tn (Rn-1)—Rn
constant pattern	T1—R1 T2 (=T1)—R2 T3 (=T1)—R3 Tn (=T1)—Rn
concentrated pattern	T1—R1 T2—R2 T3—R3 Tn-1—Rn-1 Tn (=T1+T2+Tn-1)—Rn
derived pattern	T1—R1 T2 (=part of T1)—R2 Tn (part of T1)—Rn
crossing pattern	T1—R1 T2 (R1)— R2 (T1) T3 (T2)—R3 (R2)

Task 5 Read the following paragraphs, and decide which pattern each belongs to.

1. It is apparent,(T1)/ therefore, that universities can benefit from learning

Unit 3 Developing a Logical Paragraph

about their own students' perceptions of plagiarism in order to develop appropriate strategies to promote academic integrity (R1). In light of this, (T2 = R1) / the aim of our research program is to systematically examine students' understandings of, and attitudes towards, plagiarism, with the intention of informing the institution on approaches that might promote a greater awareness of plagiarism and, therefore, prevent its occurrence (R2). This study (T3 = R2) / is exploratory in nature and will form part of a larger investigation (R3).

2. The plant (T1) / is also influenced by other living things with which it competes (R1). It (T2 = T1) / has to withstand parasites, hungry birds, and grazing or gnawing mammals (R2). Yet a plant (T3 = T1) / often needs animals to spread its pollen or scatter its seeds (R3).

3. ① Albert Einstein, one of the world's geniuses, (T1) / failed in his university entrance examination on his first attempt (R1). ② William Faulkner, one of America's noted writers, (T2) / never finished college because he could not pass his English courses (R2). ③ Sir Winston Churchill, who is considered one of the masters of the English language, (T3) / had to have special tutoring in English during elementary school (R3). ④ These few examples (T4) / show that failure in school does not always predict failure in life (R4).

4. My father's face (T1) / is rough (R1). His complexion (T2 = part of T1) / is leathery and wrinkled (R2). His nose, broken twice in his life, (T3 = part of T1) / makes him look like a boxer who has lost too many fights (R3). His mouth, unless he smiles, (T4 = part of T1) looks hard and threatening (R4). His chin (T5 = part of T1) is massive and angular (R5).

5. Urbanization (T1) / is a relatively new global issue (R1). As recently as 1950 (T2 = R1), / only 30% of the world's population was urbanized (R2 = T1). Today (T3 = T2), / more than half live in urban centers (R3 = R2).

Task 6 Rearrange the following sentences to make logical paragraphs.

1

1) There is interesting interest in natural antioxidant products for use as

medicines and food additives.

2) TOS including superpxide anion radical, hydroxyl radical and hydrogen peroxide are generated under physiological and pathological stresses in human body.

3) Antioxidant played an important role in lowering oxidative stresses caused by reactive oxygen species (TOS).

4) Vitamin C, Vitamin E and carotenoids are some of these widely used natural antioxidant.

2

1) Such treaties must be approved by a two-thirds vote of the Senate. He also negotiates with other nations less formal "executive agreements" that are not subject to Senate approval.

2) The president appoints ambassadors and other officials, subject to Senate approval, and with the secretary of state, formulates and manages the nation's foreign policy.

3) Under the Constitution, the president is primarily responsible for foreign relations with other nations.

4) The president often represents the United States abroad in consultations with other heads of state, and through his officials, he negotiates treaties with other countries.

Task 7 Fill in the blanks with the information given in the brackets.

1. A striking adaptation is found in red algae. _____(这些植物) contain, in addition to chlorophyll, pigments known as carotenoids and phycoerythrins. _____(这些颜料) are present in considerable quantities and give the red algae their characteristic color.

2. The participants were students recruited from a regional Australian university. _____(共有41名学生) (25 women and 16 men), who were either in their first or third year of study, took part across seven focus groups. _____(每一重点小组) was homogeneous with regard to discipline and

year, as issues pertinent to understanding plagiarism may be discipline or faculty specific, and would therefore impact on how students perceive plagiarism.

3. It is common for supporters of road networks to reject the models of cities with good public transport by arguing that such systems would not work in their particular city. _____ (有一种反对) is climate. Some people say their city could not make more use of _____ (公共交通) because it is either too hot or too cold.

4. In this section, we introduce a nonparametric frontier approach, DEA, for constructing a cardinally meaningful and standardized CEI. _____ (该方法) can easily address the issues of data irregularity that frequently appear in TRI data as well as the mixed measurability of the underlying variables.

2.3.2 The other cohesive devices—logical connectors

In order to connect the sentences smoothly, some other cohesive devices are also used. These devices are logical connectors which serve as signals for the meaning and structure of the text.

For example,

> In addition, body language varies from culture to culture. That is, each culture employs gestures and body movements which convey some meaning often supporting the verbal utterance. Gestures and body movements are not necessarily the same in all cultures. For example, Chinese people traditionally receive gifts with both hands to show sincere thanks whereas English people would normally only use one hand. English people regard receiving gifts with both hands as a sign of being greedy, and yet Chinese think receiving gifts with one hand impolite. Thus, teachers should, in addition to explaining how culture influences verbal language, also call students' attention to the similarities and dissimilarities between English and Chinese in body language because body language is an integral part of a culture.

In addition ... That is ... For example ... whereas ... and yet ... Thus ... in addition to ... also ... because

logical connectors

More logical connectors:

to show addition	again, and, also, besides, equally important, first (second, etc.), further, furthermore, in addition, in the first place, moreover, next, too
to give examples	for example, for instance, in fact, specifically, that is, to illustrate
to compare	also, in the same manner, likewise, similarly
to contrast	although, and yet, at the same time, but, despite, even though, however, in contrast, in spite of, nevertheless, on the contrary, on the other hand, still, though, yet
to summarize or conclude	all in all, in conclusion, in other words, in short, in summary, on the whole, that is, therefore, to sum up
to show time	after, afterward, as, as long as, as soon as, at last, before, during, earlier, finally, formerly, immediately, later, meanwhile, next, since, shortly, subsequently, then, thereafter, until, when, while
to show place or direction	above, below, beyond, close, elsewhere, farther on, here, nearby, opposite, to the left (north, etc.)
To indicate logical relationship	accordingly, as a result, because, consequently, for this reason, hence, if, otherwise, since, so, then, therefore, thus

Task 8 Read the following paragraphs and underline the logical connectors.

1. There are roughly three New Yorks. There is, first, the New York of the man or woman who was born here, who takes the city for granted and accepts its size and its turbulence as natural and inevitable. Second, there is the New York of the commuter—the city that is devoured by locusts each day and spat out each night. Third, there is the New York of the person who was born somewhere else and came

Unit 3 Developing a Logical Paragraph

to New York in quest of something. Of these three trembling cities the greatest is the last—the city of final destination, the city that is a goal. It is this third city that accounts for New York's high-strung disposition, its poetical deportment, its dedication to the arts, and its incomparable achievements. Commuters give the city its tidal restlessness; natives give it solidity and continuity; but settlers give it passion.

2. Great efforts were made to improve the fermentation yield of streptomycin. Some of its major metabolic precursors were isolated and identified some times ago. Recently, the biosynthesis pathways of streptomycin and its genetic control were described. In addition to biosynthetic pathways, fermentation conditions were studied to improve production yield. The use of batch-type feeding of carbohydrates resulted in an production yield. The use of batch-type feeding of carbonhydrates resulted in an increase of yield by 23%~24%. Moreover, the effects of carbon source consumption rate on streptomycin production were investigated. The yield when 34 g·L^{-1} of olive oil was used as the sole carbon source is about 2.0-fold higher than when starch medium was used. (张俊东等, 2018, p.70)

3. In this study, we report that G protein promotes lung cancer cell invasion. Moreover, we demonstrate that inhibition of G protein reduces the metastasis of lung cancer cells in vivo. Finally, we demonstrate that the expression of G protein is significantly up-regulated in the early stages of lung cancer. (张俊东等, 2018, p.74)

Task 9 **Fill in the gaps in the paragraphs below to see how the paragraphs are logically connected.**

1. Basically the Conservatives are seen as the party of the individual, protecting the individual's right to acquire wealth and to spend it how they choose, and so favoring economic policies which businessmen prefer, such as low taxes. They receive a lot of their party funding from big companies. _____ in the past this economic policy was coupled with a "fatherly" sense of obligation to the less fortunate in society, which meant that even though the "Big" government, which Labor set up in the post-45 era was against their principles, they did not dismantle it when they were in power. _____ the difference between the

Labor party and the Conservative party is one of degree, not an absolute. _____, neither party has stood still, and there have been substantial recent changes in both parties.

2. Warmer temperatures may decrease the number of people who die each year from cold weather. _____, in the United States, only 1,000 people die from the cold each year, while twice that many die from the heat. _____, of the ten states with the greatest number of cold-related deaths, Alaska and Illinois are the only northern states. For the most part, cold-related deaths occur during occasional cold spells in areas with mild winters where people prepare less for the cold, or during extreme events like the severe snow storm that struck Colorado in November of 1997. Global warming is unlikely to reduce either of these situations. _____ deaths due to the heat are more sensitive to temperature changes than deaths due to the cold; the difference between −20°F and −15°F, _____, has a much smaller than an increase from 95°F to 100°F.

UNIT 4

Introducing the Research Topic

1. What is the introduction to a research paper?

1.1 Introduction

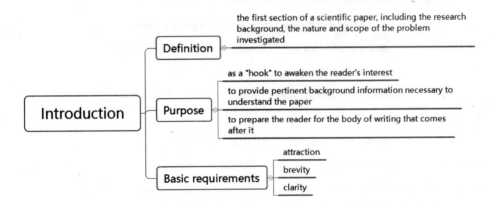

1.2 The structural layout of an introduction

The introduction of an academic paper should include the following parts: context/background information, literature review, and the purpose of the research. Sometimes, the outline of the paper is also mentioned.

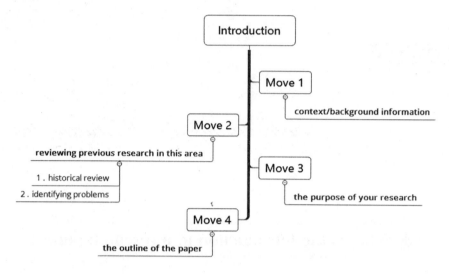

◆ 1.3 Reading activity

Task 1 Read and outline the following passage.

A hybrid financial trading support system
using multi-category classifiers and random forest

Manoj Thakur, Deepak Kumar

Indian Institute of Techonolgy-Mandi, Mandi 175001, Himacha Pradesh, India

Introduction:

Over the last few decades, the growing popularity of computing technologies and communication networks has made buying or selling of financial assets much easier and faster. This had led to ample trading opportunities to both individual investors and financial institutions, and nowadays requires nothing more sophisticated tools than a computer machine. Due to such consequence, financial securities industries have been among the fastest emerging fields in the modern economic world. The maturity of financial markets is resulting in the shaping of a more complex, nonlinear, noisy, dynamic and chaotic system [1-3]. Hence, the problem of financial market trend prediction has been a difficult job and demands new models that can capture the behavior of securities industry trends and can help to make better trading decisions. Numerous studies have been conducted to model the stock market behavior using machine learning algorithms that can learn useful models from price data. Research done in this area has led to sophisticated techniques with reduced computation time and improved the capability of systems to address the intricate problem offered in stock markets to trend prediction.

One of the most widely used learning algorithm for forecasting the trend of financial market is artificial neural networks (ANN) [14-7]. ANN has the capability of approximating any non-linear function without any prior assumptions about the model, underlying function, and the input data and thus many researchers [8-11] have applied ANNS to predict the future market trend or price. Support vector machine (SVM) [12], a structural risk minimization (SRM) principle [13] based machine learning algorithm has recently gained popularity in financial modeling than ANNS [14-16]. In the last decade, SVM has been reported to have better performance than ANNS in financial forecasting [17-19, 16] due to low generalization error as compared to empirical risk minimization techniques. Deriving features from quantitative information available in the market such as historical prices have shown promising results. Several studies [20, 17, 18, 21, 19, 22, 23] have demonstrated that implementation of SVM to forecast trends or the prices of the assets by taking technical indicators as input variables outperform the ANNS.

Deciding the appropriate feature space for SVM [16.5, 15] as an input for financial decision support system is critical due to its sensitive correlation among input variables and inherent noise of the financial time series. The low correlation of input to output or high correlation with another input may drastically affect the performance of the prediction model and may result in high generalization error in the prediction phase. Feature selection techniques try to address this problem by discovering the optimal subset of input variables. Therefore, research in the recent years is also focused on the development and use of suitable feature selection techniques to enhance the generalization capability and reducing the computation time in building the prediction model for financial markets. Various feature extraction methods, such as Principal Component Analysis (PCA), Kernel Principal Component Analysis (KPCA), Independent Component Analysis (ICA) [24], Genetic Algorithm (GA) [14] and nonlinear independent component analysis [25], have been used to identify the optimal subset of features that serve as inputs to SVMS for forecasting the market prices. Recently, Lee [26] proposed SVM based prediction model with hybrid feature selection techniques for forecasting the future direction that combines the F-score with Supported Sequential Forward Search (F-SSFS).

In the last decade, research in the area of automatic learning has opened an unprecedented possibility in developing more reliable decision support system for financial trading strategy. Various hybrid artificial intelligence tools have been developed that help to make a financial trading decision. Tsaih et al. [27] applied a hybrid AI approach that integrates the neural network technique with the rule-based systems technique to predict daily price changes in S&P 500 index futures. A decision support system was proposed by Baba et al. [28], combining neural networks and genetic algorithms for forecasting the Tokyo Stock Exchange Indexes. Though many studies for trading decision support system have shown encouraging results, most of them are evaluated based on statistical measures such as forecasting accuracy, mean squared error, precision, recall. Transaction cost is one of the most important factors that needs to be considered while evaluating the performance of a financial trading system. Most of the studies done in the area of automatic trading system have not included transaction cost while measuring the trading system performance. However, Alexander [29] and Hudson et al. [30] are reported that the performance of a trading strategy is quite sensitive to the transaction cost.

In more recent work, a hybrid neurogenetic system for financial trading was proposed by Kwon et al. [31]. A recurrent neural network (RNN) is used for the predicting the market direction and a Genetic Algorithm (GA) optimizes the NNS weights under 2-D encoding and crossover. Wen et al. [32] proposed an intelligent stock decision support system by combining the support vector regression (SVR)[33] and box theory. Both studies have been reported that automatic stock decision support system performed significantly better than buy-and-hold strategy. Above mentioned studies have concluded that the hybrid prediction model in financial forecasting performs better than the individual learning paradigm. However, the way of integration of such methods is very critical for development of such prediction models. The aim of these studies is to combine the use of different techniques to achieve better decision making system than employment of the techniques alone. Recently, Kumar et al. [17] proposed Proximal support vector machine (PSVM) based predictive model with random forest that uses a tree based ensemble technique to rank the relative importance of input technical indicators. The empirical findings suggested that random forest (RF) in combination with PSVM is superior to linear correlation, rank correlation, regression relief techniques for stock index trend prediction.

This study focuses on the development of financial trading systems which uses Weighted Multicategory GEPSVM (WMGEPSVM) [34] in combination of random forest (RF) and technical indicators. This automatic financial trading system is named as RF-WMGEPSVM. Various technical indicators and oscillators are used as input variables for WMGEPSVM to predict the trends of the market. The RF technique is applied to find the optimal set of input technical indicators for WMGEPSVM. The trading strategy gives "Buy/Hold/Sell" signals that are generated based on the historical price of the stock indices. The proposed financial trading system is tested with the NASDAQ, DOW JONES and S&P 500, NIFTY 50 and NIFTY BANK futures indices over a period of 500 trading days. The data considered for the study consist of variety of market scenarios that are witnessed during various phases (bullish, bearish and sideways) of the real financial markets. Some of the most widely used practical performance measures used in financial markets such as rate of return, percent profitability and Maximum draw-down are used to evaluate the performance of the proposed trading strategy. Performance of RF-WMGEPSVM is compared with traditional and recently developed approaches such as buy and hold investment strategy, rf-psvm [17], balanced multicategory support vector machine (BMPSVM) [35], ova-multi-class least squares twin SVM (MLSTSVM) [36] and RF in combination with BMPSVM (RF-BMPSVM) and

MLSTSVM(RF- MLSTSVM) based on these measures. Experimental findings show that the RF-WMGEPSVM system outperforms most of other strategies with respect to these matrices and is also found to be effective in bullish, bearish and sideways financial market scenarios.

The contents of this paper are organized as follows. The proposed financial trading strategy is explained in Section 2. Section 3 gives a brief introduction of RF and WMGEPSVM used in the current study. Section 4 reports the experimental findings comparison and analysis of results. Conclusions from the current study are drawn in Section 5.

(Thakur & Kumar, 2018, pp. 337 -349)

2. How do we write the introduction section?

2.1 Establishing a research context/background

The best way to establish a context is to start with the research background that the reader already knows. For example, the author could show the readers that the general research area is interesting, important, problematic or relevant in some way.

Research subject	Sentence models
interesting	① There has been growing interest in the development of _____ (research subject). ② The increasing interest in _____ (research subject) has heightened the need … ③ _____ (research subject) has become a favorite topic for … ④ The possibility of _____ (research subject) has generated wide interest in … ⑤ Much research in recent years has focused on _____ (research subject).

Unit 4 Introducing the Research Topic

(To be continued)

Research subject	Sentence models
important	① _____ (research subject) are an important and useful element in _____ (research area). ② _____ (research subject) has historically played center stage in _____ (research area). ③ _____ (research subject) has been an important part of _____ (research area) … ④ Much importance has been placed on _____ (research subject).
problematic	① _____ (research subject) continues to present a … challenge. ② The development of _____ (research subject) is a classic problem in … ③ _____ (research subject) has become the central issue in _____ (research area). ④ One of the most controversial issues about _____ (research subject) is …
relevant	_____ (research subject) has long been associated with _____ (research area/the relevant research subject).

Task 2 Fill in the blanks with the information in the brackets.

1. In the last few decades, ferroelectric (FE) thin films _____ _____ (越来越引起人们对……的关注) for the potential applications in tunable microelectronic devices, such as phase shifters, varactors and oscillators.

2. In recent years _____ (越来越多的技术领域已经开始) to use low-temperature plasmas.

3. The increasing interest in high angle-of-attack aerodynamics _____ _____ (增加了对计算工具的需求) suitable

to predict the flow field and the aerodynamic coefficients in this regime.

4. Since the early 1960s, several synthetic, degradable polymer systems _____ (已经被用作) medical implant materials.

5. In recent years, digital watermarking _____ (受到了应有的重视) from the security and cryptography research communities.

6. Bisphenol A (BPA), an important industrial chemical to which humans are exposed on a daily basis, _____ (长期以来一直和……相关) endocrine disruption in experimental animal models.

7. _____ (其中最具争议性的问题之一) about arguments involving deontic and ethical matters is whether statements of duty or right can be inferred from statements of fact or conversely.

8. _____ (近年来许多研究都集中在) various routing strategies for supporting efficient communication in point-to-point networks.

9. Many commentators have noted that sentence connectors (e.g., however) _____ (是一个重要而有用的元素) in expository and argumentative writing.

10. In the 1990s _____ (对……兴趣越来越大) in the development of electric vehicles in response to the public demand for cleaner air.

Task 3 Translate the following sentences into English.

1. 在过去的30年中,学生使用教学评估的情况稳步增加。
2. 在大多数组织的管理控制体系中,预算一直处于中心地位。
3. 近几十年来,计算机应用的任务范围有了巨大的增长。
4. 对于越来越多来自不同文化背景的学生来说,数学教育一直是美国教育的重要组成部分。
5. 对全球变暖和城市空气污染的关注已成为交通政策决策的中心问题。

2.2 Writing a literature review

A literature review is a description of the literature relevant to a particular field or topic. It should not only review the pertinent literature to orient the reader, but also evaluate the quality and findings of the research and explain how it integrates into the proposed research program. A good literature review, therefore, indicates the problem that has not been solved by the previous research, raising a relevant question:

- What is known?
- What is unknown?
- Or controversial statement of the questions

2.2.1 Previous studies

	Sentence models
previous studies	① Lots of previous studies were devoted to _____. Some of them indicate that _____ ... Furthermore, ... ② As part of this decade of research, there has been a special focus on _____. As _____ (researcher) claims _____. ③ There has been considerable research on _____. ④ Studies of _____ (research subject) have traditionally focused on _____. ⑤ A wide array of methods has been used in _____. ⑥ _____ (researchers) reviewed the earlier research examining _____. ⑦ Past studies in _____ (research area) can be reviewed with regard to _____. First, _____. The second _____. Several studies on _____. Other researchers introduced, in their studies _____.

Task 4 Fill in the blanks with the information in the brackets.

1. ① _____ （作了许多研究调查） this evaluation practice. ② Researchers such as Smith (1997) and Sedlin (1999) _____ （发展了） guidelines to help conduct teaching evaluations more successfully. ③ Aleamoni and Hexner (1980) _____ （注意到） that opinions about student evaluations vary, from reliable and useful to unreliable and useless. ④ Some _____ （声称） that many of the attempts to assess programme content and teacher effectiveness have been "ungainly and ill-defined". (Norris, 1990, p.22)

2. ① For the past three decades, _____ （大量的研究致力于检查） the role of anxiety in second language (L2) learning. ② However, as shown in Scovel's (1978) review of the literature then available, _____ （早期研究） on anxiety and L2 learning _____ （产生出矛盾的结果） regarding the relationship between anxiety and L2 achievement or performance. ③ Many researchers _____ （将这些不一致的发现部分归因于） the use of inadequate anxiety measures, such as scales of test anxiety and general trait anxiety, which do not assess an individual's responses to the specific stimulus of second language learning (Horwitz, 1986; Horwitz, Horwitz & Cope, 1986; MacIntyre, 1999). ④ Furthermore, these researchers _____ （提议） we may regard conceptualizing second/foreign language anxiety as a unique form of anxiety specific to the L2 learning context. ⑤ Since then, _____ _____ （开发了几款工具并广泛被采用于测量） this anxiety, including Gardner's (1985) French Class Anxiety Scale and French Use Anxiety Scale, and Horwitz et al.'s (1986) Foreign Language Classroom Anxiety Scale.

Unit 4 Introducing the Research Topic

Task 5 The sentences in each paragraph are not presented in their correct order. Number the sentences in a logical order.

1.

a. Jevons (1990) and Smart (1995) forecast the increasing access to and use of computers in schools.

b. Green and Barnes (1991) cite a number of specific applications in the training of accountancy students ranging from drills to simulation exercises.

c. Schmidt (1982) identified three uses in the classroom: as the object of a course, as a means of support, and as a means of providing instruction.

d. There is general agreement that computers will continue to enjoy a central place in education.

2.

a. Since vocabulary is regarded as central to language learning, students are supposed to memorize all the new words and expressions on which they will be tested.

b. Therefore, they treat all the new words and expressions with an equal amount of time and care, and students tend to treat all the new items as active vocabulary.

c. Teachers rarely consider which items may be students' active vocabulary and which items may be students' passive vocabulary.

d. The majority of English coursebooks in China provide students with long lists of vocabulary attached to the end of the texts.

2.2.2 Research problems

After a general review of the past studies, some problems should be identified to indicate the need for more investigation. Sometimes, adverbs like "however", "nevertheless", "but" are used as transitional words so that readers will turn their eyes to the existing problems, limitations or controversies of the particular research field.

	Sentence models
Identifying problems	① However, neither of these studies _____ (research problem). ② However, the previously mentioned methods suffer _____ (research problem). ③ Although _____ (research subject) has been investigated extensively, _____ (research problem). ④ Although _____ (research subject) has been widely investigated, very few practical applications have been identified for _____ (research subject). ⑤ Unfortunately, _____ (research subject) suffer from certain limitations, _____ (research subject) have motivated many researchers to explore … ⑥ If these results could be confirmed, they would provide strong evidence for _____ (research subject). ⑦ Prior research efforts do not identify _____ .

Task 6 Translate the following sentences into Chinese.

1. However, with a mean follow-up of only 2 ~ 3 years these trials were unable to establish any effect on the colorectal cancer.
2. Nevertheless, these attempts to establish a link between secondary smoke and lung cancer are at the present controversial issue.
3. However, the copolymers of diphenols and PEG have so far not been studied as medical implant materials.
4. However, neither of these studies provides any descriptive evidence of the actual positions of sentence connectors in academic texts.
5. Unfortunately, the current treatment options for articular cartilage repair suffer from certain limitations.

Unit 4 Introducing the Research Topic

Task 7 Translate the following parts in the brackets into English.

1. However, the precipitation driving force _____
   _____(尚未完全确定)。

2. However, _____(上述方法主要存在一些局限性) mainly concerning the treatment of the vortex wake formation and its interaction with the body.

3. Although the cationic ring-opening polymerization of SOCs _____
   _____(进行了广泛的研究), only a low molecular weight (MW) polymer _____(得到了) and the MW _____(无法进行控制).

4. Although synthetic poly (amino acid) _____(被广泛调查),
   _____(但很少有实际应用) have been identified for these polymers.

◆ 2.3 Determining the purpose of the research

The last part of the introduction is to inform the reader of the general purpose of the research.

	Sentence models
The purpose of the research	① The purpose of this research was to further investigate … ② In this paper, we propose an alternative distributed approach … ③ In the present paper, we report on a preliminary study of … ④ The objective of the present study was to … and to investigate … In this work we attempt to … ⑤ Recently, we found that … In this paper … are discussed in detail. The present work is aimed at studying … ⑥ Realizing the importance …, an attempt has been made to develop … in this study.

Task 8 Translate the following parts in the brackets into English.

1. _____ (本工作将最后模型的应用范围扩大到) asymmetric, body-vortex cases, thus increasing the range of flow patterns that can be investigated. _____ (此外,还努力改进) the numerical procedure to accelerate the convergence of the iterative solution and to get a better rollup of the vortex lines representing the wake.

2. _____ (本研究的目的是进一步研究和表征) the Sanitary Engineering Research Laboratory reactor system.

3. _____ (在本文中,我们提出了一种可替代的分布式方法), where the local admission decisions are made independently at the edge routers of each domain.

Task 9 Translate the following into Chinese.

1. In the present paper, we report on a preliminary study of sentence connector position in a sample of twelve published articles.

2. The present study, in taking a new approach to the study of academic writing tasks, attempts to provide some preliminary answers to these questions in the hope that other researchers will build on this beginning.

3. Based on the assumption that learners' attitudes toward a language might affect their learning of that language, this paper reports on a study which examined Chinese students' attitudes toward Singapore English.

◆ 2.4　Forming the outline of the paper

Sometimes, the outline of the paper which shows how the paper is organized is presented in the introduction. This part is optional. Read the following example.

Unit 4 Introducing the Research Topic

The paper is organized as follows: Section 2 presents the framework of Adaptive Fuzzy Fitness Granulation. An auto-tuning strategy for determining width of membership functions (MFs) is also presented in the section; by which the need of exact parameter setting is eliminated, without affecting the rate of convergence. This approach is called Adaptive Fuzzy Fitness Granulation With Fuzzy Supervisory (AFFG-FS). In Section 3, the proposed algorithm is tested on three traditional optimization benchmarks with four different dimensions. In Section 4, the recovery of the PN sequence from a received watermarked signal using the proposed approach is illustrated. Some supporting simulation results and discussion thereof are also presented in the section. Finally, conclusions are drawn in Section 5. (Davarynejad et al., 2010: 719)

Task 10 Read the following paragraphs to see how the paper is organized.

1. This paper is divided into three parts. The experimental set-up is described in the first part. Then, the microstructure evolution of the alloys under irradiation is reported, in particular characteristics of the solute clusters. Finally, the effects of dose, flux and chemical composition are discussed. (Meslin et al., 2010, p.137)

2. The remainder of this paper is structured as follows: Section 2 presents background material, Section 3 describes our experimental setting, Section 4 presents the hypotheses, Section 5 discusses the method and Section 6 presents the results, and Section 7 provides a summary and conclusions.

3. The four parts of this report will discuss (1) a technological overview of DVD, utilizing a comparison of CD vs. DVD technologies, (2) the construction of a DVD, (3) current applications utilizing DVD, and (4) projected sales and revenues of DVD devices. The technological overview section will use a comparison of current CD specifications vs. DVD

specifications to convey the advances made possible using DVD. The construction section explains the manufacture of a DVD to show the physical advantages of DVD for data storage and retrieval. The section covering current applications examines the five current formats for DVD specifications and how they are currently being used. Finally, the sales and revenues section includes forecasts of DVD sales and distribution, based upon current sales and technology release.

UNIT 5

Describing Research Methods

1. What are the research methods?

1.1 Introduction

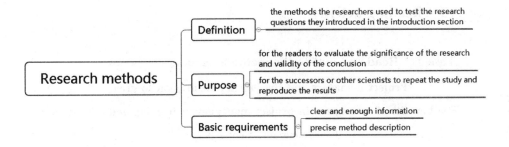

1.2 Structure of methods section

The methods section includes many small parts with subtitles. Some are optional, and others are obligatory. However, most of the scientific papers contain the following five aspects: experimental designs, subjects or sample selection, materials, procedures, data collection and analysis.

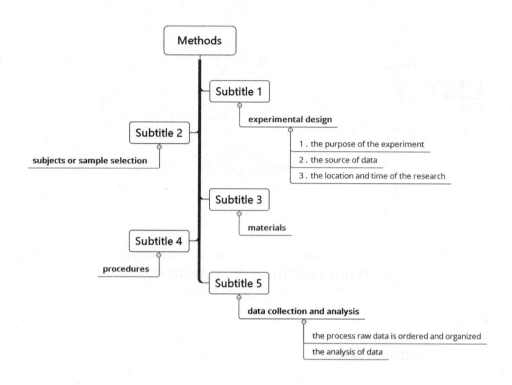

1.3 Reading activity

Task 1 Read and outline the methods section.

Project managers and the journey from good to great:
The benefits of investment in project management training and education

Jalal Ramazani, George Jergeas[1]

Department of Civil Engineering, University of Calgary,

2500 University Drive NW, Calgary, Alberta T2N 1N4, Canada

Methodology

1. Questions

This study aims to answer the following questions: How can project management education and training turn technical engineers into great project managers? What more must the education system do to help good project managers evolve to become great?

2. Respondents

The study targeted project managers and project engineers working in the oil and gas sector in Calgary who were able to discuss their experiences in detail. Participants were selected using a combination of two sampling procedures. The study began with convenience sampling; informants were first contacted by telephone or email, informed of the nature and purpose of the study and invited to participate. Those who indicated interest were asked to arrange a time for an interview, which would last approximately one hour. After data was generated from the first two interviews, the process of additional sampling was guided by the principles of theoretical sampling (Glaser, 2008) to ensure that only those project managers who were active and also had responsibilities in a project environment were included. Table 1 shows the demographic characteristics of the participants in this study.

3. Analysis

Applying the grounded theory approach and constant comparison method of analysis (Glaser and Strauss, 1967), the data was collected and analyzed simultaneously. Using the principles of theoretical sampling, it was confirmed that all interviewees had in-depth insight about the project. Analysis of the data started with the first two interviews, aided by standard software for qualitative analysis, namely NVivo. A group of twenty-nine project managers were interviewed, composed of 8 females and 21 males. After analyzing data the result was reviewed with a group of project managers using a focus group. In this phase, a small group of participants gathered to discuss the results of the interview analysis under the guidance of a facilitator (researcher) who often played a detached role (Klenke, 2008). Three focus groups were held with thirteen project managers.

4. Validation

To increase credibility of results, information-rich cases were selected for in-depth study as well as different sites for maximum variability (Giacomini and Cook, 2000; Mays and Pope, 2000; Patton, 2002).

Table 1
Demographic characteristics of the participants

Characteristic	Value	Frequency	Percent
Gender	Male	21	72
	Female	8	28
Education	Bachelor	18	62
	Master	8	28
	PhD	3	10
Job level	Project manager	16	55
	Senior project manager	4	14
	Project engineer	9	31
Age group	30–34	2	7
	35–39	1	3
	40–44	5	17
	45–49	9	31
	50–54	4	14
	55–59	5	17
	60–64	3	10
Years of experience	1–5	0	0
	5–10	2	7
	10–15	5	17
	15–20	9	31
	20–25	9	31
	25–30	4	14

The study also used maximum variation in order to identify important common patterns (Maycut and och Morehouse, 1994). We also attempted to overcome one of the downsides of theoretical sampling, limited variation between chains of similar informants, by actively aiming to interview project practitioners with diverse roles and positions. Triangulation for this study was established through focus groups supplemented by member checking methodologies. While the focus group sessions allowed for the verifying and mapping of critical findings, supplementing the focus groups with member checking enhanced the depth of inquiry (Guba & Lincoln, 1994).

(Ramazani & Jergeas, 2015, pp. 41 –52)

Unit 5　Describing Research Methods

2. How do we write the methods section?

◆ 2.1　Presenting experimental designs

The experimental design may begin with the purpose, the source of data or the location and time of the research, and then followed by an overview or the design of the research. This section should be short, and it is important that you do not provide too much detail of the procedure used. This ensures that the design is clear and concise, and avoids any unnecessary repetition.

> • Sample 1
>
> ① In order to look at faculty-student interaction at 2-year institutions, I conducted a quantitative study using data gathered from the Transfer and Retention or Urban Community College Students (TRUCCS) Community College Student Survey. ② The survey was designed to explore factors promoting the retention and perseverance of urban community college students. ③ Among the 47 questions on the survey, items examining students' demographic characteristics, college course-taking patterns, engagement in campus activities, and attitudes and views are included. (Chang, 2005, p.780)
>
> 　　The purpose: to look at faculty-student interaction at 2-year institutions
> 　　Kind of research: a quantitative study
> 　　Source of data: data gathered from the Transfer and Retention or Urban Community College Students (TRUCCS) Community College Student Survey
> 　　The survey design: Sentence ② and ③

• Sample 2

① This is a focus group study, where <u>our aim was to collect qualitative data</u> by engaging groups of students in an informal group discussion "focused" on their perceptions of plagiarism. ② <u>Our study aimed to</u> place students (who are typically aware of the rhetoric surrounding plagiarism) in the position of experts, whose knowledge and experience is essential to advance the theoretical discussion on student perceptions of plagiarism. ③ <u>It was intended,</u> as suggested by Madriz(2000), that the interaction among group participants would reduce the interaction between the moderator and the individual members of the group. ④ In this way, <u>the role of the moderator was to</u> actively facilitate discussion among the participants, by encouraging students to discuss their views with each other as opposed to directing them to the facilitator. (Gullifer & Graham, 2010, pp. 463 – 481)

  Kind of research: <u>qualitative study</u>

  The purpose: <u>to place students ... in the position of experts, whose knowledge and experience is essential to advance ...</u>

  Method: <u>The interaction among group participants would reduce the interaction between the moderator and the individual members of the group.</u>

  Supposed result: <u>In this way, the role of the moderator was to actively facilitate discussion among the participants, by encouraging students to discuss their views with each other as opposed to directing them to the facilitator.</u>

Task 2 Translate the following sentences into English.

1. 本实验旨在探讨在医学背景下中国大学生对英语需求的认知。
2. 调查是在上海某工业自动化研究中心下属的国家实验室进行的。

3. 正如之前的比较研究所示,这项研究的目的是确认计算机词典比纸质词典更能提高学习者的查找行为。
4. 两项研究是在西南大学进行的,针对年龄从19岁到22岁不等的本科生,主修西班牙语以外的其他领域。
5. 为了研究这一问题,本文采用了定量的研究设计,旨在探索相关变量之间的相关性的研究。

Task 3 Translate the following paragraphs into Chinese.

1. The qualitative approach we employed enabled us to glean a wealth of information about: (1) student perceptions of their development in writing in English, (2) student perceptions of other outcomes or "by-products" not in English writing but related to course participation, and (3) teacher observations of changes in students during the writing courses.
2. This study was conducted in two phases, the objective being to first identify those characteristics most common to the successful hire of effective project managers, from the perspective of IT recruiters. Once identified, the study sought to determine preference of these characteristics from the point of view of corporate IT executives nationwide.
3. The current investigation involved sampling and analyzing six sites to measure changes in groundwater chemistry. The sites were selected from the London Basin area, which is located in southeast of England and has been frequently used to interpret groundwater evolution.

Task 4 The following sentences are in a scrambled order. Rearrange the sentences into a logical order.

1. Table 1 shows the demographic characteristics of the participants in this study.
2. The study began with convenience sampling; informants were first contacted by telephone or email, informed of the nature and purpose of the study and invited to participate.

3. Participants were selected using a combination of two sampling procedures.
4. The study targeted project managers and project engineers working in the oil and gas sector in Calgary who were able to discuss their experiences in detail.
5. After data was generated from the first two interviews, the process of additional sampling was guided by the principles of theoretical sampling (Glaser, 2008) to ensure that only those project managers who were active and also had responsibilities in a project environment were included.
6. Those who indicated interest were asked to arrange a time for an interview, which would last approximately one hour.

◆ 2.2 Describing methods

The methods already established in the field should be referred to. Novel methods must be described so that the research or experiment can be replicated by another researcher. The statistical methods should also be described.

- Sample 1

① The KIFCM (Kernel Intuitionistic Fuzzy c-means) algorithm has been shown to have good performance by the previous studies. ② However, its results are not stable since it is highly dependent on the initial membership values and centroids. ③ Therefore, this study is the first study which intends to improve this algorithm by employing metaheuristic algorithms. ④ Each dataset has unique characteristics, and most clustering algorithms are limited for some particular data types. ⑤ Thus, combining the KIFCM algorithm with a metaheuristic algorithm will deliver a more general and robust algorithm.

Describing previously used methods and its problems: Sentence ① and ②

Unit 5 Describing Research Methods

> Presenting novel method: Sentence ③
> Giving reasons why a particular method is used: Sentence ④ and ⑤

The next are some useful expressions for describing methods.

Describing previously used methods	① These methods have a problem of ... ② A number of techniques have been developed to ... ③ Different methods have been proposed to classify ... ④ There are three main types of study design used to identify ... ⑤ Due to ..., we used elements of several research approaches from different disciplines, including ...
Presenting the novel method	① The utilization of ... has been extensively reported in the literature. ② Therefore, in the present study, ... are constructed ... ③ A case study approach was used to allow a ... ④ The ... used in the present study was ..., because ... ⑤ This method is particularly useful in studying ... ⑥ This paper presents a novel approach in the implementation of ... ⑦ As one of the most popular methods of ..., the ... has been widely used in ..., particularly in ... ⑧ In this paper we used ... method, with the aim of exploiting ... ⑨ Ours was a mixed methodology approach incorporating both qualitative and quantitative aspects.

Task 5 Read the following paragraphs carefully and see how research methods are described.

1. The methods of early fusion try to concatenate the different types of features into a unified feature representation. These methods have a problem of large dimensionality. Therefore, many sophisticated methods are developed, which includes the fusion of similarity measure and the learning of multi-view subspace.

2. The standard cuckoo search algorithm or CSA has the remarkable advantages such as simplicity and easy avoidance of local optima in comparison to other optimization algorithms. However, it has some major

drawbacks such as slow convergence and low accuracy. Hence, The convergence rate and accuracy of standard CSA should be enhanced in advance before implementing in clustering problem.
3. As discussed above, the proposed ICMPKHM clustering algorithm is a combination of the improved cuckoo search (ICS) algorithm and MPSO (modified particle swarm optimization) algorithm. Using both ICS and MPSO for solving KHM (the K-Harmonic Means) problems has the two significant advantages of leading it to global optima and fast convergence. The improved CSA (The standard cuckoo search algorithm) procedure and hybrid clustering algorithm are discussed below.
4. ICAKHM is regarded as a novel method which was designed based on a combination of K-harmonic means algorithm and a modified version of the imperialist competitive algorithm (ICA).

2.3 Describing the experimental sampling method

When writing the methods section, it is important for the writer to describe the characteristics of the participants that were used within the experiment. Thus, selection criteria are sometimes necessary. Also the basic demographic profiles of the sample population such as age, gender and even nationality might be explicitly described. If animals are the subjects of a study, species, weight, strain, sex and age should be included.

- Sample 1

① Participants were 68 full-time students at a university in Japan who were native Japanese speakers learning English as a foreign language. ② They were aged from 18 to 25; 47 students were female (69.1%) and 21 were male (30.9%). ③ About one-third of them were majoring in English literature, another third had not yet chosen their majors (because they did not have to until their third year), and the other third of the students were majoring in various fields such as philosophy, psychology, and sociology.

Unit 5 Describing Research Methods

④ All of them had at least 6 years (an average of 8.36 years) experience learning English in junior high school and high school in Japan. ⑤ The participants shared similar educational and cultural backgrounds, so these intervening variables were controlled in the study. ⑥ Their level of English proficiency varied, but most were in the intermediate level judging from the scores they reported for some standardized tests (for example, about a third reported their TOEIC scores, and their average was 697). (Baba, 2009:193)

The above paragraph gives a general description of the participants. They were Japanese university students who had the similar educational background. Their lexical proficiency in writing summaries in English was tested.

Task 6 The following sentences are in a scrambled order. Rearrange the following sentences into a logical order.

1. To be included in the sample, individuals must have been employed in a for-profit organization employing at least 100 people located in the United States or Canada (but outside of Quebec).
2. The final target sample consisted of 2,583 CMA Canada members and 13,712 IMA members.
3. We gathered data via a web-based survey of managers holding senior positions in medium- to large-sized organizations.
4. The sample came from the 2003 membership directory of CMA Canada and the 2004 membership directory of the Institute of Management Accountants (IMA).
5. In addition, we selected potential respondents based on holding the positions of Vice President, Chief Financial Officer, Controller, Director of Budgeting or Division Manager.
6. We chose these criteria to ensure that the target group of organizations was large enough to have formal budgeting systems and so that managers we

contacted would have considerable experience in establishing and using budgets.

Task 7 Translate the following paragraphs into Chinese.

1. Three groups of EFL students majoring in English in China participated in the present study. Only English majors were recruited due to the concern that students otherwise might not have sufficient English writing experiences to provide rich information regarding their writing anxiety experiences.

2. All subjects were postgraduate international students at Loughborough University. The criteria for selection for all subjects was that they had not previously lived in or visited the United Kingdom for more than two weeks, they were not nationals of the European Union, and they were not native English speakers.

3. The participants were 40 parents: 21 recent Chinese immigrants and 19 non-immigrant Caucasian-Canadians, each from a different family. These families had a combined total of 46 children, 21 Chinese and 25 European-Canadian. Only one father took part in the interview and only one family involved both parents in the interview; mothers represented the rest of the families. The families lived in a medium-sized Canadian metropolitan city. The Chinese families, who originated from Taiwan, Mainland, and Hong Kong, had immigrated to Canada within the last 10 years, the majority (18) within the last 5 years. Members of the non-immigrant families were all Caucasian, having been born and having always resided in Canada.

Task 8 Read the following excerpts taken from experimental papers and decide which part of method they belong to.

1. Participants consisted of 70 students in total (27 first-, 30 second-, 11 third-, and 2 fourth-year students) enrolled in two courses designed for non-native speakers of English at a large Canadian university. The majority

of the participants (n = 47) were enrolled in an introductory writing course, whereas the remaining 23 were registered in a communication skills component. (Radia & Stapleton, 2008, p. 12)

2. Participants were split into three conditions and given a verbal memory task. In Condition 1 participants were told to use the counting mnemonic to remember the words, in Condition 2 the method of loci mnemonic and in Condition 3 the participants were told to use no strategy. The dependent measure was the number of correctly recalled words.

3. We require a sample that enables us to assess the leadership style of top management and the control choices made by those managers. We collect questionnaire data from profit center managers from a cross-section of firms in the service and manufacturing sectors of the Netherlands. These managers report to the CEO of the firm and are considered to be the most appropriate respondent to reflect on leadership style and control system choice of top management. The managers are selected as follows. We first identify a sample of service and manufacturing firms that reflect the regional distribution of firms throughout the Netherlands and is consistent with the ratio of service and manufacturing firms in the Netherlands. These firms were then contacted and asked to participate. Each firm is visited to ensure that they are of the required size and have a profit center structure. We only include firms that have at least three profit centers of a reasonable size (i.e. greater than 100 employees). We require firms to be sufficiently large to warrant the implementation of formal management control systems. It is important that the systems in place can be used for performance measurement and for planning and control. We interview one randomly selected profit center manager in each firm. In addition to visiting each of the firms, we offer to provide a performance measurement seminar to all respondents. This method of obtaining participation results in an excellent response rate. Of the 170 firms contacted, more than 75% agree to participate. This results in a sample of 128 profit centers. (Abernethy et al., 2010, p. 5)

4. The students were all music majors, first- or second-year students at an American conservatory. To be placed in this course, they had either scored between 540 and 575 on the Test of English as a Foreign Language (TOEFL) or they had completed a year-long intermediate English as a Second Language (ESL) course at the same institution the previous year with a grade of B- or better, after scoring at least 500 on the TOEFL. One class (the control group) consisted of 16 undergraduates from East Asia (Korea, Japan, China), and the other (the experimental group) contained 15 similar students. Each class had only one male student. Although students were not randomly assigned to the classes, there was no indication of systematic differences between them, and both classes were taught by the same teacher-researcher. (Chandler, 2003, p. 269)

◈ 2.4 Describing research materials or instruments

Materials refer to the items the researchers use in carrying out the method. They can be equipment, specimens, natural or man-made substances, computer or mathematical models, questionnaires, etc. Exact technical specifications of materials and the standard terminology are provided. Read the following paragraphs and pay attention to the terminology the writer used.

• Sample 1

Cytochrome C from bovine heart was used as a model protein and was purchased from Sigma—Aldrich, St. Louis, MO, USA. Sephadex G 25 Coarse grade was obtained from GE Healthcare Ltd., Uppsala, Sweden. All other chemicals were purchased from Sigma—Aldrich. Dry dichloromethane was prepared by refluxing over calcium hydride for one hour; constant boiling fractions were collected and stored over 4Å molecular sieves under N_2. Anhydrous dimethyl formamide was stored after purchase over 4Å molecular sieves under N_2.

Unit 5 Describing Research Methods

Technical terms:

Cytochrome C from bovine heart 细胞色素 C[牛心]

Sephadex G 25 Coarse grade 葡聚糖凝胶 G-25 粗级

Sephadex 葡聚糖

Dichloromethane 二氯甲烷

Calcium hydride 氢化钙

Anhydrous dimethyl formamide 无水二甲基甲酰胺

molecular sieves 分子筛

- **Sample 2**

  Two sets of questionnaires were used in the study in an attempt to (1) identify the participants appropriately and (2) illustrate participants' L-S behaviors. A prewriting questionnaire (see Appendix A) based on those used by other researchers (Cumming, 1988; So, 1997) employed a five-point Likert-like scale. The questionnaire was written in English and sought demographic information on students' age, gender, and educational background, as well as the students' English study background, self-evaluations of their level of English proficiency, and Chinese and English writing expertise. A 10-minute post-writing questionnaire (see Appendix B) was administered to each participant at the end of the second writing session. The post-writing questionnaire was designed to elicit participants' retrospective self-reports of their L-S behaviors in their L2 writing processes. (Wang, 2003, p.349)

The above paragraph gives a detailed description of the materials (questionnaires) used in the research.

Task 9 Read the following paragraph and see how research materials are described.

Two questionnaires were developed for the survey, based on two earlier survey instruments by Taylor & Hussein (1985) and Guo (1989). The questionnaires were translated into Chinese, piloted and modified according to the feedback from 10 respondents: 6 medical students and 4 faculty members from the university. The questionnaire given to the medical students consisted of 23 questions grouped in five sections, the topics of which were: (1) demographic information; (2) the importance of English in college and professional careers; (3) perceived needs and problems of language skills; (4) the activities needed in freshman-year language courses; (5) suggestions for the development of course content and materials as well as demographic information. The faculty questionnaire included 16 questions grouped in four sections, which were parallel to those in the version given to the students except that no demographic information was gathered.

Task 10 Translate the following parts in the brackets into English.

1. The response sheet _____ (由13道李克特5分量表 5-point Likert scale 题组成) per stimulus.

2. As for the post-tests, _____ (编制了多项选择题) in which the participants were asked to choose a Korean equivalent among 4 alternatives.

3. In this study, I _____ (用了结构式访谈), with an open-ended questionnaire to allow variation in responses.

4. _____ (采取了个案研究办法) to capture the complexities of the phenomenon.

5. _____ (在确定的15项标准中), recruiters found Experience (87%) and Education (70%) to be the most valued, with PMP (Project Management Professional) certification only moderately important at 52%.

Task 11 Underline the research materials or instruments used in the following sentences.

1. A 32-item questionnaire was mailed to 3,258 IT managers and executives, asking them, through a 7-point Likert scale, to identify the relative

importance of each of the 15 criteria in their screening of PM candidates for their organizations.

2. The substrate used in the present study was chromium coated sodalime glass slides, because cadmium and zinc were found to stick poorly over glass.

3. A multiple-choice test which can measure the receptive knowledge of the words was considered appropriate to measure the retention of the words gained incidentally from reading, since the probability that the participants can gain word knowledge at the production level at one exposure is very low. The immediate test and the delayed test contained the same items, but in a scrambled order.

4. The two-page response sheet (see Appendix C) was adapted from Kayaer & Bhundhumani (2007). Each participant received an identical response sheet to record his or her responses to the same questions for both stimuli. The response sheet included questions regarding each woman's estimated weight and asked participants to rate the woman's weight based on her height being either 63 in (1.6 m) or 67 in (1.7 m). The researchers asked participants to rate their perception of the women's levels of happiness and success in life. The response sheet asked participants to judge how popular, friendly, judgmental and outgoing each woman was. The researchers added additional questions regarding how often the participants thought the women dieted and exercised.

◆ 2.5 Narrating or explaining the experimental procedure

The procedure of the research is the narrative of the experiment. It explains what you have participants do, how you collect data, and the order in which steps occur. It may list the main steps that make up the process. These steps can be described one by one in a chronological or logical order. Read the following paragraphs and pay attention to the underlined part.

• Sample 1

　　Strain surrounding dislocations or other defects in a crystalline material may be revealed by acid etching. <u>The first step</u> is to place the acid into the beaker so that it just covers the polished mineral surface. <u>After about 6 hours</u> the pit etching should be distinct. One must <u>then</u> wash and dry the sample and, if it is non-metallic, coat it with the enhancing deposit, usually a 100-Å gold or similar inert material. <u>Following this procedure</u> the strain concentration regions (resulting from the presence of lattice defects) may be viewed as etch pit clusters by examination with the scanning electron microscope.

　　The above paragraph is arranged in a chronological order. Phrases like "the first step", "after about 6 hours", "then", "following this procedure" are used to indicate the steps of acid etching.

• Sample 2

　　The experiment was conducted in a quiet room of the university department. Participants attended two experimental sessions individually; the sessions were held on two different days with a one-week interval between. Each session took about 2 ~2.5 hours (i.e., each student spent a total of 4 ~ 5 hours in two sessions). Prior to each task, individual participants were given instructions in how to perform it. I sat silently in the room while the tasks were carried out. Every task had an approximate time limit, which was based on a pilot study. However, the participants were allowed to extend the time limit. They were asked not to spend too much time on any one task, in particular, the summary writing task (e.g., no more than one hour). The order of the tasks was randomized to reduce task-order effects. Ten different orders of the tasks were devised and randomly assigned to the participants. (Baba, 2009, p.195)

　　The above example precisely shows how the experiment was carried out. The writer first describes the place, and then the participants and their tasks.

Unit 5 Describing Research Methods

Task 12 Read the following paragraph and underline the research procedures.

In the main session, the participants of the paper group were provided with Sisa Elite English-Korean dictionaries in the classroom. Meanwhile, the participants of the computer group participated in the experiment in a computer lab where they could access the same version of the dictionary through the computer. First, the students were instructed to read the printed text for a comprehension test. The vocabulary test was not announced so that the condition was conducive to incidental vocabulary learning. There was no time limit, but they were advised to read the text within 15 minutes. They were allowed to consult dictionaries as much as they needed. However, they were asked to underline the words they looked up in the dictionary. After they finished their reading, the reading comprehension test was administered. Then, an unannounced vocabulary test was given. Finally, the participants were asked to respond to the questionnaire. Two days after the main session, a delayed unannounced vocabulary test was given in the presence of the researcher.

Task 13 Translate the following sentences into Chinese.
1. The experiment consisted of the pretest, the main session and the delayed test. All the sessions were held during the regular class time and in the regular classrooms with the cooperation of an instructor in charge of the two classes in May 2003.
2. Before reading the text, the pretest was administered to measure the pre-knowledge of the target words in the presence of the researcher. Based on the result, 14 target words that more than 90% of the respondents did not know were chosen.

2.6 Collecting and analyzing the data

The last step in the methods section is the analysis of data. It is a process in which raw data is ordered and organized with the goal of highlighting useful information. It is essential for the writer to think critically what the data does and does not contain. Read the following example.

① All data from interviews, archival records, and observation summaries were kept in manual folders for frequent reference. ② Data were analyzed in a three-phase process to ensure that all information was consistent across different sources, to establish the temporal order of events, and to surface relations among the variables of interest in our control framework. ③ In the first phase, we analyzed interview transcripts for similarities and differences across interviewees. ④ We then investigated alternative information sources (archival records, observation summaries, and photographs) to highlight any inconsistencies requiring further examination. ⑤ In the second phase, we studied the chronological order of the data in order to establish a clear delineation of the accounting practices and control systems both prior to and after adoption of the lean strategic initiatives. ⑥ In the third phase, we reexamined the evidence to surface the relations among the variables providing the foundation for our theoretical model. (Kennedy & Widener, 2008, p.305)

General description of data: Sentence ①
Analysis of data: Sentence ②
First phase: Sentence ③ and ④
Second phase: Sentence ⑤
Third phase: Sentence ⑥

Unit 5 Describing Research Methods

Task 14 Translate the following Chinese in the brackets into English.

Each of the 773 essays _____ (转录) by the researcher for use with the CLAN computer program (MacWhinney, 1995). _____ (这个程序通常用于) for the analysis of spoken child language, but _____ _____ (这个转录系统) was adapted for written texts according to the suggestions in the CLAN manual. The essays were transcribed using standard orthography. _____ (转录完成后), the program was used to tag the lexical category and morphological inflections of each word. The mean length of the essays is 175 words (S.D. 88.4). _____ (在标记过程的第一个阶段), the program assigned likely codes for each item. The texts were _____ (然后) handchecked by the researcher for mistakes in the machine coding and ambiguous items such as WH words, which can be interrogative pronouns, relative pronouns or adverbial clause markers. (Dudley, 2002, p.314)

Task 15 Fill in the blanks with the proper forms of the given words.

1. Only the 14 target words in the vocabulary tests _____ (score) by the researcher. With respect to the pretest, a correct answer for each vocabulary item received a score of 1. A half point _____ (give) to the answer.

2. As suggested by Hayes (2000), each transcript _____ (read) several times to identify content topics, that is, similar threads interwoven throughout all the transcripts. This coding of the data continued for each transcript until no new categories _____ (find). After this initial trawl, patterns and commonalities among the categories _____ (identify and group) into proto-themes.

3. Once completed, the theme's final form _____ (construct, name and define). This _____ (do) by referring back to the literature, deriving information that would allow inferences to be made

from the focus groups.

4. The data _____ (computer-analyze) using an SPSS program; in two questionnaires, percentages _____ (determine) for all questions. Chi-square, t-tests, and ANOVA analyses _____ (conduct) in order to determine the perceptions of English language needs of medical students and their faculty and to compare the perceptions held by the various groups.

UNIT 6

Presenting Results and Discussing Major Findings

1. What are the research results & discussion?

1.1 Introduction

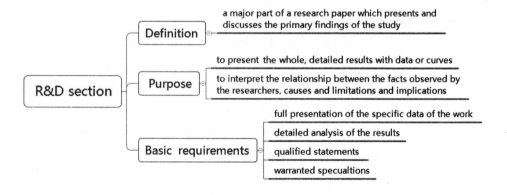

1.2 Moves in writing R&D section

The R&D section should include the following moves:

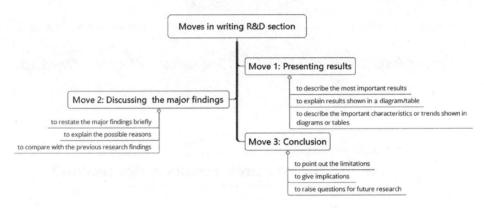

1.3 Reading activity

Task 1 The following is the discussion part of one paper. Read and pay attention to the functions of different parts.

In this paper we have presented two methods (EML and EML+) to suppress the forgetting of unused classes in an online incremental learning setup. Since the classes of data in a real-time online stream are not necessarily uniformly distributed, they can create a block of absence. During this absence, an unused class is not learned and the model is prone to forget it. Our methods use competitive updates in traditional RLS that focus on the importance of the data points in the stream during the learning process. This shrinks the blocks of absence of a class while keeping the important information available for the learning process.

We compared our techniques using four baseline models and achieved better results than the baseline techniques. We discuss several options for incremental learning, some of which have been used for online or incremental handwriting recognition. As we wanted to show the usability of the proposed models not only for handwriting recognition, but also for various other problems, we chose to test a spectrum of datasets. We evaluated results on 8 datasets that varied in the number of classes, features and sample sizes. In all of the applications our techniques achieved a good trade-off between the immunity for forgetting of unused classes and the general accuracy of the model.

From the results we can see that both of our methods are superior to the original RLS in regard to the immunity to forgetting of the unused classes, and they both are capable of maintaining the general accuracy of the models. The general accuracy is very important for the model to be able to achieve good results even when there are no blocks of absence of classes, and our methods do not influence the learning process of all the other classes. In some rare cases, however, the general accuracy was lower than in the original models. We believe that this is due to the nature of the data and the importance of each sample for the learning process. The learning process of all classes is slightly slowed down compared to a case in which all classes are learned at the same time. Especially in EML, the learning is more competitive than in EML +. This follows our assumption, since by using more samples in EML + we were able to improve the general accuracy of the model. Further we point out that if we focus on the last samples' accuracy, the results improve as well. This corresponds to our theory that worse results are caused by lack of data due to the competitive nature of the model. On the other hand, the more competitive the learning is, the more it is, in general, immune to forgetting. Again, there are some rare cases when this is not completely true; but since in both EML and EML + the learning is competitive, we can see that using such learning is superior to learning all samples, as in RLS. We can note that in all cases our methods surpassed RLS and in the vast majority of the results the improvement was very significant.

Given these findings we can state that our approaches outperform baseline techniques significantly in cases where some classes are used only on rare occasions compared to the rest of the classes. This gain in performance is reduced when distribution over classes is more or less uniform. However, this reduction is not critical and both methods lead to comparable or even superior results when there are no blocks of absence of classes present. Nevertheless, the main application of our models is on handwritten gestures recognition. Consequently, we might suppose that the distribution of handwritten gestures of users in a real-world setting is not uniform and that several gestures are used only on rare occasions.

In our future work we want to explore the problem of forgetting in cases where even though our methods did indeed improve the original results, the accuracy during the forgetting phase was still not acceptable. It might seem that for these datasets either the models or the competitive learning process itself is not quite suitable. As a part of this research we want to investigate the application of our EML and EML + to optimization techniques other than RLS.

2. How do we present research results and discuss the major findings?

Sometimes the Results and Discussion sections are combined into one section because some authors are likely to make comments directly after they show each result or they discuss them one by one until all the results have been presented.

2.1 Presenting research results

The purpose of a result section is to present and illustrate the results of the research. Results are usually presented both in diagrams and texts. Diagrams are supported by texts. They usually include tables, graphs or charts.

Unit 6 Presenting Results and Discussing Major Findings

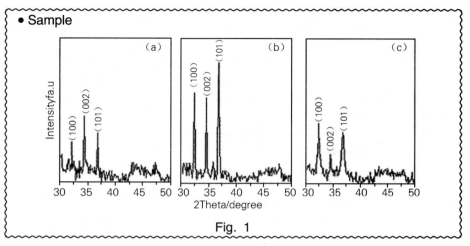

Fig. 1

Fig. 1 shows the X-ray diffraction pattern of the samples grown at different temperatures for 15 min. As seen in Fig. 1, the samples after ammoniation are hexagonal wurtzite GaN with lattice constant of a = 0.3186 nm and c = 0.5178 nm, and the diffraction peaks located at 2θ = 32.3°, 34.5°, and 36.7° correspond to (1 0 0), (0 0 2) and (1 0 1) planes, which are consistent with the reported values for bulk GaN.

There are many ways of presenting results. For example, we can describe the tendency, compare among groups, point out the correlations between variables or display the proportions in a chart.

The next are some useful expressions for writing results.

Showing a tendency	① The table shows the changes in the number of ... over the period from ... to ... ② This table shows the changing proportion of X and Y from ... to ... ③ The graph, presented in a pie chart, shows the general trend in ... ④ As can be seen from the graph, the two curves show the fluctuation of ... ⑤ The number of ... remained steady from ... to ... ⑥ There is an upward trend in the number of ... ⑦ A considerable increase occurred from ... to ... ⑧ This is a cure graph which describes the trend of ... ⑨ There was a ... drop in ... ⑩ ... showed a tendency to increase over the three year period.
Comparing among groups	① The difference between X and Y lies in ... ② There are a lot similarities between ... and ... ③ These findings match with those from ... ④ ... decreased year by year while ... increased steadily. ⑤ Changes in X and Y were compared using ... ⑥ The average scores of X and Y were compared in order to ... ⑦ Data from this table can be compared with the data in Table 4.6 which shows ...
Pointing out the correlations between variables	① The coefficient of correlation was found to be significant at ... level. ② The results ... are consistent with ... ③ ... was highly correlated with ... ④ ... does not agree with ... ⑤ The correlation between X and Y was tested using ... ⑥ A positive correlation was found between ... and ... ⑦ No significant correlation was found between ... scores and the ... scores ...

Unit 6 Presenting Results and Discussing Major Findings

(To be continued)

Displaying the proportions	① The pie chart above shows the proportion of different categories of ... ② From the chart, it can be seen that by far the greatest demand is for ... ③ Of 150 patients who were sent invitations, 81 returned the reply slip, of whom 60 agreed to ... ④ By the end of the survey period, data had been collected from 64 individuals, 23 of whom were ... ⑤ 70% of those who were interviewed indicated that ... ⑥ Almost two-thirds of the participants (64%) said that ... ⑦ The majority of those who responded to this item felt that ... ⑧ When asked whether ..., 90% of the respondents reported that ... ⑨ Of the 148 patients who completed the questionnaire, just over half indicated that ... ⑩ Just over half of those who answered this question reported that ...

Task 2 Complete the following sentences according to the Chinese in the brackets.

1. The students' cultural awareness _____
   (呈现上升趋势) over a month's training.

2. Enrollment in the English program _____
   _____ (快速下降) from 2002 to 2004.

3. There was _____ (16%的降落) in the smoke concentration in the North of England between 2003 and 2001.

4. Smoke concentration in the North of England _____
   (2003年比2001年低很多).

5. After one year, cars of Make A performed quite well in the test of petrol consumption _____ (而) the Make B cars performed badly.

6. The performance of the students _____ (与……有着紧密联系) their length of exposure to the target language.

7. _____（相关系数）was found to be significant at the .001 level.

8. This _____（与……相一致）earlier findings suggesting that personal characteristics are not related to attrition and teaching.

9. These findings _____（与……相匹配）those from a larger study in which the same supplementation program increased birth weights by an average of 224 g in the months July to January.

10. Of the study population, _____（90个受试者）completed and returned the questionnaire.

Task 3 Translate the following sentences into English.

1. 三十二个人提交了问卷。
2. 近三分之一的参与者喜欢使用智能手机上网。
3. 年龄与从事技能工作的工人的经验密切相关。
4. 该值与标准值不一致。
5. 在过去的三年里，物价呈现出上涨的趋势。

Task 4 Translate the following sentences into Chinese.

1. The results obtained for paraffin wax, ice and lead are consistent with the published values.

2. The results show a clear difference in the petrol consumption and reliability of the two makes of car. With two exceptions, Make A was consistently more economical and reliable than the average, whereas Make B was, with three exception, less reliable than average.

3. As the graph shows, there was an upward trend in TV sales. In February, TV sales rose from 1,200 to 1,400 sets. In March, they remained constant at 1,400 sets. In the next two months, they increased steadily, from 1,400 sets to 1,800 sets. However, the next two months saw a steady fall and they were back at 1,200 sets in August. After this dramatic fall, there was a substantial rise in the following months and the TV sales

rose in December to finish the year at 2,200 sets.

4. Figure 1.1 displays the scores on the four subtests for the non-immersion and immersion students of English. Students in the English immersion programme performed significantly better than those not following the programme on all four Modern Language Association tests.

5. The serious problem of health costs in the U.S. may be understood from Table 1 where the cost of health services in the U.S. is compared to that of several other countries. As we see from the table, the figure for the U.S. is almost twice the value of the second highest cost, that of Japan, and considerably higher than that for all other developed or developing nations.

2.2 Discussing major findings

Discussions (sometimes including conclusions) are based on the information contained in the results section. The major purpose of this part is to show the relationships among the observed facts. It is used to interpret the data, explain the possible reasons, compare the present research with other researches, evaluate its value, point out the limitations and raise questions for future research.

The next are some useful expressions for writing discussion section.

Summarizing the major findings	① The results of this study show/indicate that … ② Prior studies that have noted the importance of … ③ An initial objective of the project was to identify … ④ The first question in this study sought to determine … ⑤ The present study was designed to determine the effect of … ⑥ The most interesting finding was that …

(To be continued)

Explaining possible reasons	① A possible explanation for this might be that ... ② Another possible explanation for this is that ... ③ This result may be explained by the fact that ... ④ There are, however, other possible explanations. ⑤ These relationships may partly be explained by ... ⑥ These results are likely to be related to ... ⑦ It seems possible that these results are due to ... ⑧ This rather contradictory result may be due to ...
Comparing with the previous research findings	① Comparison of the findings with those of other studies confirms ... ② This also accords with our earlier observations, which showed that ... ③ These results reflect those of Smith et al. (1992) who also found that ...
Stating the limitations	① A limitation of this study is that ... ② Being limited to X, this study lacks ... ③ The major limitation of this study is the ... ④ This study was limited by the absence of ... ⑤ One issue with the current study was that ... ⑥ The findings in this report are subject to at least three limitations. First, ... ⑦ However, these findings are limited by the use of a cross-sectional design. ⑧ The number of tourists surveyed was quite small. ⑨ Only three sets of samples were tested ...
Giving implications/ making conclusion	① This provides some explanations as to why ... ② An implication of this is the possibility that ... ③ One of the issues that emerges from these findings is ... ④ Some of the issues emerging from this finding relate specifically to ... ⑤ This combination of findings provides some support for the conceptual premise that ...

Unit 6 Presenting Results and Discussing Major Findings

Task 5 Read the following passages and decide the functions of each paragraph.

1. The reasons for such a strong correlation can be various. One interpretation for such a gender difference is that females have talents for language learning while males have talents for mathematics and sciences. Such a view has been reported by quite a few researchers such as Allen and Valette. The alternative interpretation is that the male students who major in English are not the best students in the whole group since, according to the Chinese tradition, the best male students usually go into the science stream. Following this argument, we will challenge the explanation that females have greater talents for language learning.

2. Evaluating the significance of a result falls into the scope of discussing. The significance may be theoretical or practical. By evaluating its theoretical significance, you try to link the result to the previous findings and existing theories to see whether your result is the same as the previous ones or in conflict, and to see whether your result is in support of the existing theoretical assumptions or against them.

3. The key finding of the study is that the HP participants switched to their L1 more frequently than the LP participants did while composing the two writing tasks. This finding contradicts previous L-S studies such as Woodall's (2000). This disparity might be attributable to the different manipulation of coding L-S data. (Wang, 2003, p.375)

4. In general, all participants switched languages frequently and to about the same extent (from 30% to 45% of their thinking sequences) while composing in the L2. This finding suggests that L-S was common to the HP and LP participants, and it might have facilitated their writing processes while they were composing. (Wang, 2003, p.375)

5. Limitations of this approach include the fact that we scored only harms. All drugs have some benefits to the user, at least initially, otherwise they would not be used, but this effect might attenuate over time with tolerance and

withdrawal. Some drugs such as alcohol and tobacco have commercial benefits to society in terms of providing work and tax, which to some extent offset the harms and, although less easy to measure, is also true of production and dealing in illegal drugs. Many of the harms of drugs are affected by their availability and legal status, which varies across countries, so our results are not necessarily applicable to countries with very different legal and cultural attitudes to drugs. (Nutt et al, 2010, p.1565)

6. In conclusion, we have used MCDA to analyze the harms of a range of drugs in relation to the UK. Our findings lend support to the previous work in the UK and the Netherlands, confirming that the present drug classification systems have little relation to the evidence of harm. They also accord with the conclusions of the previous expert reports that aggressively targeting alcohol harms is a valid and necessary public health strategy. (Geim et al., 2001, p.739)

7. This study has some implications for teaching idioms. Firstly, it is important to inform learners of the different metaphoric themes in the target culture. Secondly, more attention should be paid to idioms without NL equivalents. Thirdly, overt comparisons can be made to show learners which idioms can be transferred from their NLs and which idioms are likely to cause interference, thus taking advantage of the positive transfer while avoiding the negative transfer. Fourthly, while helping learners realize the absurdity of the literal meanings of some English idioms, this study encourages them to tackle the semantics of idioms as a problem-solving task, and teaches them strategies for dealing with figurative language to take advantage of the semantic transparency of some idioms.

8. In conclusion, the architecture developed in the present study allows for the correct classification of different types of nerve fibres. A multi-level structure is needed, in which supervised and unsupervised methods are used, in this order at different levels. This scheme improves classification accuracy and opens the possibility of its use in automated tasks. We demonstrated that the identification and classification of different types of nerve fibres can be carried out with a reduced number of characteristics.

Unit 6　Presenting Results and Discussing Major Findings

Task 6　Complete the following sentences according to the Chinese in the brackets.

1. The results _____ (表示) that the usage of regularity markers did not decrease as the regular language arts students became older, nor did the usage of power markers increase.

2. In comparison to the test topic they use more regularity markers and fewer power markers, _____ (可能因为) the power markers interrupt the flow.

3. These findings _____ (是可以理解的) because the initial annealing temperature dictates the state of conformation structures.

4. _____ (可以推测) that the adhesion between the toner film and the cotton fabric was lower than for the other fabrics and that the increase in friction in the wet state was sufficient to remove the toner from the fabric.

5. These results _____ (与……相符) the findings of Casadio et al.

6. These data _____ (与……一致) earlier findings showing that the best alloying addition is trivalent Ga.

7. Ethical principles and values _____ (对……很关键) undertaking actions that lead to sustainability.

8. _____ (与……相比) our earlier work, in this paper we established a control interaction between heterogeneous groups and we introduced potential based cohesion and separation forces to regulate intervehicle distances, without affecting the stability properties of the ground group.

9. _____ (与……一致) the results of other published studies in this area (e.g., Hasher & Chromiak, 1977), instructing subjects to remember the frequency information did not influence frequency judgement performance.

10. _____（这个方法的局限性）include the fact that we scored only harms.

Task 7 Translate the following sentences into Chinese.

1. The results of the analysis show that the most important sustainability criteria are those that relate to behavior, followed by business factors. Within these behavioral criteria, ethics, competitive intelligence, intrinsic motivation and self-efficacy are particularly important.
2. Several different damage mechanisms, such as wear, plastic deformation and rolling contact fatigue, may be responsible for the development of out-of-round wheels and rail corrugation.
3. These results suggest that untrained octopuses can learn a task more quickly by observing the behavior of another octopus than by reward and punishment method.
4. By comparing the simulation results of the two types of adhesion force models with the experimental results, it is found that these adhesion force models can effectively represent the experimental results.
5. The views of experts might be subject to biases resulting from their career paths, academic training or experience. However, this is also a strength of the method, which was based on the views of people with experience in a range of areas with different cultures.
6. Our findings lend support to the previous work in the UK and the Netherlands, confirming that the present drug classification systems have little relation to the evidence of harm. They also accord with the conclusions of the previous expert reports that aggressively targeting alcohol harms is a valid and necessary public health strategy.

Unit 6 Presenting Results and Discussing Major Findings

◆ 2.3　Using hedging words

　　It is commonly believed that academic writing is factual, conveying facts and information. However, tentative language is also used especially in the discussion and conclusion section of the scientific paper. This kind of technique is known by linguists as a "hedge" or "vague language". Writers use such kind of language to show their scientific attitude toward their research work. Read the following passage and pay attention to the underlined parts.

　　(L1 and L2—the first and second language; L-S—language-switching; LP—low levels of English proficiency; HP—high levels of English proficiency)

　　In general, all participants switched languages frequently and to about the same extent (from 30% to 45% of their thinking sequences) while composing in the L2. This finding <u>suggests</u> that L-S was common to the HP and LP participants, and it <u>might</u> have facilitated their writing processes while they were composing. The key finding of the study is that the HP participants switched to their L1 more frequently than the LP participants did while composing the two writing tasks. This finding contradicts previous L-S studies such as Woodall's (2000). This disparity <u>might</u> be attributable to the different manipulation of coding L-S data. In Woodall's study (2002), L-S data were defined as "any use of the L1 while engaged in the L2 writing process" (p.15). In operation, Woodall identified a switch as a sequence starting from an utterance in the L1 to the next utterance in the L2, whereas I, through a careful analysis of what preceded and followed a switch, identified a L-S sequence as a problem-solving behavior prompted by an utterance in L2.

　　Regarding the reasons why the HP participants <u>might</u> have attained more switches than the LP participants did while composing the tasks in L2, I found that the LP participants' L-S was mostly initiated as they attempted to (1) reduce their content-generation processes by merely "getting ideas down", (2) simplify their writing production at levels of lexis, syntax and semantics, (3) consult dictionaries for words, and (4) retrieve grammatical rules. To compensate for their L2 linguistic deficiencies in their writing processes, the LP participants often concentrated on direct translation from their L1 into the L2 to perform their L2 writing. Composing their writing tasks in this way might have helped them overcome writing difficulties without exerting much mental effort.

In contrast, the HP participants tended to switch from the L2 to their L1 for problem-solving and ideational thinking. For this purpose, the HP participants devoted their switching to attending to overall aspects of language generation and high-level writing processes, such as formulating and monitoring contextual meaning, consulting discourse plans, and considering task constraints and intended readers. Consequently, their writing intentions that pursued high-level writing goals seemed to involve their setting "a more difficult task for themselves than is faced by novice writers" (Bereiter, Burtis & Scardamalia, 1988, p.262). This could explain why the HP participants frequently switched languages when they confronted idea generation or rhetorical problems while they were composing. In addition, the finding that there was no significant difference between the L-S frequencies of the HP participants across the two writing tasks seems to imply that the HP participants' L2 proficiency assisted them in bridging the linguistic differences in the two languages and activating the mental operations to regulate their writing processes. Their ability to strategically switch to the L1 might create a genuine opportunity for them to achieve their writing intentions by transforming their knowledge flexibly and steadily across the two tasks. Hence, this result suggests that learners' L2 proficiency could affect their capacities of how and for what purposes they might switch to their L1 to manipulate their writing processes while composing in L2. (Wang, 2003, p.375)

Unit 6 Presenting Results and Discussing Major Findings

Language used in hedging:

Verbs	seem, tend, look like, appear to be, think, believe, doubt, be sure, indicate, suggest, believe, assume
Modal verbs	will, must, would, may, might, could
Adverbs/adjectives	certainly, definitely, clearly, probably, possibly, perhaps, conceivably, certain, definite, clear, probable, possible
Nouns	assumption, possibility, probability
Adverbs of frequency	often, sometimes, usually
Clauses	It might be suggested that ... It may be possible ...

Task 8 Read the following sentences and underline the tentative words and phrases used.

1. If this latter trend were to follow that of government health costs, the trend would be approximately given by the dotted line portion of curve b in the figure.
2. It is likely that such severe turbulence affected the automatic landing indicators which had failed or displayed faulty data during descent to the Toledo airport.
3. The final judgment of the matter may be difficult or impossible because of the lack of good test data that could be obtained from other portions of the severely damaged aircraft.
4. In the case of building roads connecting cities, there might be some costs involved with every road intersection.
5. The weather condition at the time suggests that the most likely cause of the damage to the rudder was due to both vertical and horizontal air turbulence.
6. It is possible of course that other industries with a different complex of speed jobs and skilled jobs may produce entirely different results.
7. Their L1 switching for rhetorical concerns may involve relatively complex and interactive mental operations to explore variables between lexis and context environments in a contrastive rhetorical pattern.

8. However, the repeated L-S in their verbalizations in searching words could be considered as an output condition that in the long term could help them to build an internally associative system between the two languages.
9. Application of simple statistical techniques like interpolation of state/regional level inventories to obtain gridded data is likely to cause misrepresentation of emissions at sub-regional scales, which can get accumulated to the global scale in the models.
10. The location of emission hot spots seems to correlate to the densely populated rural areas, once again emphasizing the contribution of rural bio-fuel emissions.
11. We might have overestimated the latent period duration before an effect of aspirin on death due to colorectal cancer.
12. A similarly large change in the weight on drug-specific damage would be needed, from about 4% to slightly more than 70%, for tobacco to displace alcohol at first position. And an increase in the weight on harm to users from 46% to nearly 70% would be necessary for crack cocaine to achieve the overall most harmful position.

Task 9 Below are some statements which may sound too definite. Rewrite them to make them sound more tentative.

a. Use tentative verbs such as "seem", "appear", "suggest", "tend".
1. In this case, the prediction of accident rates between age groups is confirmed.
2. The HP participants switched from the L2 to their L1 for problem-solving and ideational thinking.
3. The lack of exposure to the target language is the reason for the students' poor listening ability.

b. Use modal auxiliaries such as "can/could", "may/might", "should".
1. The reasons for this erratic pattern are the age distribution of the children or the relatively small number of women in the sample.
2. These results are explained by considering the voltage distribution on 230

Unit 6   Presenting Results and Discussing Major Findings

   kv insulators during freezing conditions.
3. These discrepancies are due to lack of purity in the substance.
4. Other variables, for which there are no objective data, influence the frequency of the outcomes.
5. The amount and type of graphic presentation reflect the designer's view of potential readers.

UNIT 7

Writing an English abstract

1. What is the research paper abstract?

◆ 1.1 Introduction

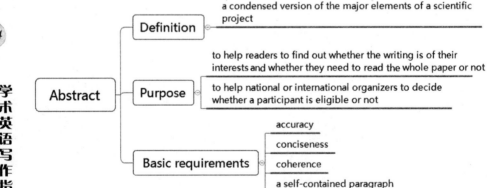

1.2 The general format of an abstract

1.2.1 Types of abstracts

Generally speaking, there are two major types of abstracts: descriptive and informative. A descriptive or indicative abstract usually indicates the type of information found in the work. It only provides key information elements of the paper. However, an informative abstract provides the reader with an overview of the study and highlights the findings and results of the research.

The following chart shows the differences:

A descriptive abstract	An informative abstract
describes the major points of the project to the reader	informs the audience of all essential points of the paper
briefly summarizes the purpose, methods, and scope of the research	presents the context and importance of the research question which is addressed, the methods used, the principal findings and the major conclusions derived from the study
short and self-contained	specific and sometimes quantitative
under 100 words or less	no more than 10% of the length of the entire report
appropriate for review articles	appropriate for research papers

1.2.2 Structure of an abstract

Abstract structure follows the same order as the structure of the paper (IMRD).

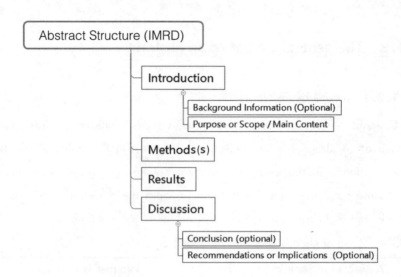

◆ 1.3 Reading activity

Task 1 Contrast the following abstracts and tell the differences between the descriptive abstract and the informative abstract.

1. ① The main purpose is to provide a personalized view in the usage as well as the organization of digital library materials. ② In this paper, we describe three skills, active reading, personalized retrieval, and personalized filtering, which are considered essential to construct a personalized information environment in the digital library.

2. ① The present study describes the level of faculty-student interaction on 2-year college campuses, examines student characteristics correlated with faculty contact, and considers how interaction may differ among racial subgroups of students. ② Using data collected from the Transfer and Retention of Urban Community College Students (TRUCCS) survey, a sample of 2,500 students informed this research. ③ The findings reveal generally low levels of interaction, and especially with Asian American/Pacific Islander and Latino students. ④ Having positive perceptions of the college environment and interacting with other members

of the institution, from students to academic counselors, grow the strongest positive association with faculty contact among all racial subgroups of students. ⑤ Prominent among the differences is the negative relationship between perceiving racial difficulties and interacting with faculty for Asian American/Pacific Islander students. ⑥ The findings provide insight in how to increase and enrich faculty interaction on these campuses to better retain underrepresented students in the educational pipeline.

Task 2 Read the following three abstracts and try to figure out what elements are included in these abstracts.

1. ① This study investigated the impact of aspects of the lexical proficiency of EFL students on their summary writing in English (L2) by controlling for the impact of a range of linguistic abilities in English and Japanese (L1). ② Sixty-eight Japanese undergraduate students wrote two summaries of English texts in English. ③ Their English lexical proficiency, English reading comprehension, English proficiency, knowledge of Japanese vocabulary and writing proficiency in Japanese as well as the length of summaries were assessed. ④ Multiple regression analysis of the data showed that the effect of L2 lexical proficiency as a whole on summary writing performance was not pronounced compared to the effect of reading comprehension and the length of summaries. ⑤ However, the ability to write definitions made a unique contribution over and above the other variables including reading comprehension and the length of summaries. ⑥ It is suggested that different aspects of L2 lexical proficiency have a differential impact on EFL learners' summary writing, and that two factors in particular (the structure of semantic network of words, and the ability to metalinguistically manipulate words) may constitute the construct of summary writing in L2. (Baba, 2009, p.191)

2.　　　**International Conference on Information Sciences,**
　　　　　　Machinery, Materials and Energy
　　　　　　　　（ICISMME 2015）
　　Dynamic Inverse Based Controller for a Hypersonic Flight Vehicle
　　　　　　　　Lindong Zhao, Shengjing Tang
　　　Key Laboratory of Dynamics and Control of Flight Vehicle,
　　School of Aerospace Engineering, Beijing Institute of Technology,
　　　　　　Beijing 100081, China ajyzzld@163.com

Keywords: hypersonic vehicle; sliding mode control; Feedback linearization

Abstract: ① A dynamic inverse based controller is designed for the longitudinal dynamics of a generic hypersonic vehicle. ② This model is strong nonlinear, multivariable coupling and includes uncertain parameters based on its high speed, lager aerodynamic load and rapid changing flight area. ③ After feedback linearization of original model to get dynamic inverse linear model, optimal control method is used to develop controller to follow height and velocity commands. ④ Simulation studies demonstrate that this controller is capable to follow height and speed change commands rapidly and accurately with certain robustness. (Zhao & Tang, 2015, p.361)

3.　　　　　　**JOURNAL OF AIRCRAFT**
　　　　　　Vol. 51, No. 1, January–February 2014
　　Inspection Intervals Optimization for Aircraft Composite Structures
　　　　　　　　Considering Dent Damage
　　　　　　　　Xi Chen, He Ren & Cees Bil

① Many probability techniques have been proposed, but the inspection intervals for composite structures have not been comprehensively addressed. ② The present study focuses on the most frequent damage type, dent, and uses probabilistic approaches to analyze statistical characteristics of the damage based on maintenance data from a Chinese airline. ③ Dent sizes are considered from three dimensions: the damage diameter, the damage depth, and the diameter/depth ratio. ④ The life-cycle strength of a composite structure is obtained by Monte Carlo simulation, and the probability of failure is quantified corresponding to different inspection intervals. ⑤ Maintenance cost is introduced, as another criterion, to optimize inspection intervals from both safety and economy. ⑥ This method enables the dent damage to be assessed quantitatively, which can facilitate engineers from airlines or manufacturers to evaluate the damage tolerance of the composite structure and adjust their related inspection schedules flexibly. (Chen, Ren & Bil, 2014, p.303)

2. How do we write an English abstract?

◆ 2.1 Introducing the research topic

This section mainly introduces the purpose of the study and the subject matter the research paper is dealing with. However, some abstracts may begin with background information to explain the significance of the study in question, or to establish a theoretical basis or to define a key term.

Abstract	Sentence models
Background information (optional)	① _____ (research subject), but/yet/however _____ (the related problem) ② (while/although) _____ research problem, (yet) _____ (the present problem)
Purpose	① The goal/aim/purpose of the study/research/paper is to _____ (research subject). ② This study/research/paper aims to _____ (research subject). ③ In this paper/study, we aim at _____ (research subject). ④ This research is designed to determine/measure/evaluate _____ (research subject). ⑤ The author intends/attempts to outline the framework of / obtain some knowledge of _____.

(To be continued)

Abstract	Sentence models
Main content of the study	① The article/paper/study presents/examines / focuses on / advocates/ discusses/develops/proposes / holds that / gives detailed explanation for _____ (research subject). ② _____ (research subject) is investigated. ③ We have investigated _____ (research subject). ④ This paper describes/presents _____ (the argument) within _____ (a theoretical context).

Task 3 Read the following sentences and decide what function each one has in the abstract.

1. Many probability techniques have been proposed, but the inspection intervals for composite structures have not been comprehensively addressed.
2. Visible watermarking is a widely-used technique for marking and protecting copyrights of many millions of images on the web, yet it suffers from an inherent security flaw—watermarks are typically added in a consistent manner to many images.
3. The overall goal of this study is to clarify the nature of Japanese students' first language (L1) writing experience and instruction in high school to help university second language (L2) English writing teachers understand their students' needs.
4. The purpose of this paper is to develop an organizational learning framework to support the strategic management process.
5. This study investigated the language learning strategy use of 55 ESL students with differing cultural and linguistic backgrounds enrolled in a college Intensive English Program (IEP).
6. Water condensation, a complex and challenging process, is investigated on a metallic (Zn) surface, regularly used as anticorrosive surface.

Unit 7 Writing an English abstract

Task 4 Translate the following underlined parts into Chinese.

1. <u>The aim of the paper is to develop</u> (i) operational performance indicators from the inefficiency score and (ii) a benchmarking procedure adapted to the network structure of the banking group under study.

2. <u>We have investigated</u> the use of walking plaster casts in the management of seven diabetic patients with long-standing, chronic foot ulcers.

3. <u>This study concerns</u> the cognitive effort expended and the difficulties experienced by undergraduate students as they took notes and wrote a text based on a lecture given in French, their primary language (L1), and in English (L2).

4. <u>This paper focuses on</u> organizational learning and innovation in international joint ventures (IJVs). Organizational learning addresses how organizations adapt to their environments, develop new knowledge, and then achieve competitive advantage.

5. <u>This paper explores</u> the potential role of family socioeconomic factors in school achievement outcomes at two separate periods in the life course—early in childhood and during late adolescence.

Task 5 Translate the following Chinese in the brackets into English.

1. _____ (这份报告的目的是讨论) the value of radiation.

2. _____ (这项研究是为了确定) whether the growing season water balance could be manipulated through planting geometry.

3. _____ (本文发展和检验了对……的假设) about the characteristics of organizations and their environments that favor the proliferation of detailed job titles to describe work roles.

4. _____ (本研究旨在评估) the role played by information technology (IT) in organizational learning (OL) considered as a process of knowledge creation and determined by the interaction of stocks and flows variables.

5. ① _____ (几乎没有相关的研究) what happens during

writing center (WC) sessions to how student writers revise their subsequent drafts. ② _____（这文献上的空白）is particularly evident concerning second language (L2) writers who come to the WC for assistance. ③ _____（这项研究是为了填补这一空白），exploring the connection between WC interaction and revision by L2 writers.

6. ① _____（很少有人注意到）the role of leadership characteristics in the organization design literature despite significant evidence of its importance in explaining firm behavior. ② _____（本研究开发并测试了一个模型来评估）the effects of leadership style on three control choices that are considered integral elements of a firm's management control system; namely the delegation choice, the use of planning and control systems and the performance measurement system.

◆ 2.2 Presenting the used methods

This part briefly indicates the research design, materials, tools and methodology.

	Sentence models
Method/ approach	① _____ (the research method/approach) can be briefly described/called / applied to / based on _____.
Formula	① The formula is verified by _____ (research method). ② The formula is derived from _____ (research method).
Test	① The test was carried out on _____ (research method). ② The test is demonstrated by using _____ (research method).
Data	Data for _____ (research subject) was obtained using _____ (the research method).

Task 6 Fill in the blanks with the proper forms of the given words.

1. A method _____ (require) (a) to aggregate the inefficiency scores of individual branches to evaluate the regional groups and (b) to integrate the differences in environment into the evaluation procedure.

2. A theoretical framework _____ (propose) based on three virtually complementary perspectives by integrating international production, demand, and contemporary ICT-based theory.

3. An exploratory case study in a pure service environment _____ (describe) that illustrates the value of the framework.

4. Participants _____ (train) on a secondary task that allowed us to measure their cognitive effort while they performed two other main tasks in both languages, namely (1) listening and taking notes on the main ideas of the lecture, and (2) writing a text based on their notes.

5. Students' scores in TOEFL exam including 4 sections (listening, writing, speaking, reading) _____ (take) as a criterion for second language learning. Data is analyzed by using ANOVA test.

6. Data for the study _____ (obtain) using qualitative research methods, including in-class observation (field notes), videotaping, interviews, and collection of documents.

7. In this study, we _____ (apply) a unique method to predict the magnitude of interactive forces exerted between a globular protein and PEG-grafted matrices.

8. An in-vitro haloduracin production system _____ (use) to examine the biological impact of disrupting individual thioether rings in each peptide.

Task 7 Underline the method part of the following abstracts.

1. **Growth and Characterization of $Cd_{1-x}Zn_xTe$ Thin Films Prepared From Elemental Multilayer Deposition**

Rajiv Ganguly[a], Sumana Hajra[a], Tamosha Mandal[a], Pushan Banerjeeu[b], Biswait Ghosh[b]

$Cd_{1-x}Zn_xTe$ is key material for fabrication of high-energy radiation detectors and optical devices. Conventionally it is fabricated using single crystal growth techniques. <u>The method adapted here is the deposition of elemental multilayer followed by thermal annealing in vacuum. The multilayer structure was annealed at different temperatures using one to five repetitions of Cd-Zn-Te sequence. X-ray diffraction pattern for the multilayer with five repetitions revealed that annealing at 475°C yielded single-phase material compared to other annealing conditions. EDX spectroscopy was carried out to study the corresponding compositions. Photoluminescence properties and change of resistance of the multilayer under illumination were also studied.</u> The resistivity of the best sample was found to be a few hundreds of Ω cm. (Ganguly et al., 2010, pp. 4879 –4882)

2. This study explores the relationship between language and communication skills and patterns of success and failure in the cross-cultural adjustment of Japanese university students. <u>Seven interpersonal communication skills which were selected by Ruben and Kealey as important to cross-cultural adjustment were examined: empathy, respect, role behavior flexibility, orientation to knowledge, interaction posture, interaction management, and tolerance for ambiguity. Besides these skills, language was taken into consideration as a major component influencing Japanese intercultural communication. The behavioral assessment method developed by Ruben was utilized to measure communicative performance and behaviors of Japanese university students who visited the United States for 4 weeks for their English training. In order to assess the language skills of these individuals, listening, speaking, structure and written expression, and vocabulary and reading comprehension skills were measured.</u> At the end of their stay in the United States, the dimensions of culture shock, psychological adjustment, and interactional

effectiveness were examined. Comparisons of pre- and post-test measures indicated that six out of the seven communication behaviors observed in the Japanese students did not predict success or failure in adjustment to the United States. Only ambiguity tolerance yielded correlation with culture shock. However, speaking and listening skills were closely correlated with interactional effectiveness. (Hiroko, 1985, p.247)

◆ 2.3 Stating the results of the study

The result part mainly reveals some of the important findings in your research. These findings should be summarized and interpreted.

	Sentence model
Results	① The research results/findings indicated/showed/suggested _____. ② It is/was _____ (research result) that _____. ③ Findings are that _____.

Task 8 Translate the following sentences into Chinese.

1. The results indicated that writing processes were more effortful than notetaking.
2. Findings showed that listening, writing, structure and reading mean scores of students with different learning styles was different significantly.
3. The findings suggest people have various feelings and attitudes toward cell phone usage.
4. The study found that the students preferred to use metacognitive strategies most, whereas they showed the least use of affective and memory strategies.
5. Results suggest a significant, positive and strong relationship between organizational learning and financial performance.
6. The findings suggest specific ways for teachers to draw on students' strengths in terms of their literacy background to help them bridge the gap between their L1 and L2 writing skills.

Task 9 Translate the following Chinese in the brackets into English.

1. _____（方差分析结果表明）less proficient L2 learners switched to their L1s more frequently than more advanced learners (P = 0.004), and that more difficult tasks increased the duration of L1 use in L2 writing (P≤0.001).

2. _____（结果表明）all participants used their L1 while writing in their L2 to some extent, although this varied among conceptual activities.

3. _____（这些结果说明）that it is important to recognize both the unity and diversity of executive functions and that latent variable analysis is a useful approach to studying the organization and roles of executive functions.

4. _____（单一语言条件下的结果显示）differences in areas devoted to language processing such as the Superior Temporal Gyrus.

5. _____（我们的发现进一步表明）that knowledge acquisition is necessary to progress from relational level to internal level.

6. _____（案例研究的结果支持了）the proposition that specific social network structures are associated with different barriers to organizational learning.

7. _____（结果证明）that the nanowires are single-crystal GaN with hexagonal wurtzite structure and high-quality crystalline, having the size of 30~80 nm in diameter and several tens of microns in length with good emission properties.

8. _____（研究结果显示）that the students who cited unconventional sources appeared to be unaware of their ideological agendas.

2.4 Making discussion or drawing conclusions

At the end of an abstract, conclusions are drawn based on the results obtained, mainly on the significance of the research. It is important to point out its originality, value or implication. Sometimes, limitations are also mentioned.

Unit 7 Writing an English abstract

	Sentence models
Conclusion	① In conclusion, we state that ... ② In summary, it may be stated that ... ③ From our experiment, we concluded that ... ④ The author has satisfactorily come to the conclusion that ...
Implication	① The studies we have performed showed that ... ② The research we have done suggests that ... ③ The pioneer studies that the authors have attempted indicated that ... ④ The investigation carried out by ... has revealed that ...
Value	① Our work involving studies of ... prove to be encouraging.
Originality	① All our preliminary results shed light on the nature of ... ② The author's pioneer work has contributed to our present understanding of ... ③ This fruitful work gives explanation of ... ④ The research work has brought about a discovery of ...
Limitation	Laboratory studies of ... did not furnish any information about ...

Task 10 Translate the following Chinese in the brackets into English.

1. _____(研究结论是) that the correct judging and optimal operation of the essential factors will enhance the effectiveness of strategic management in general.

2. _____(本文的结论是) it is essential for teachers and teacher educators to develop the capability to engage in expansive learning through tackling ill-defined problems in boundary zones.

3. This paper fulfills an identified information/resources need and _____ _____ (提供实际帮助) to an individual starting out on an academic career.

4. This study _____(奠定了基础) which future studies will be built.

5. The present study _____(为进一步研究提供了一个

起点) in the international manufacturing sector.

6. This study _____ (提供历史背景) recent developments in public sector reporting and accountability in Australia, particularly the (re)introduction of accrual accounting, and provides insights into the nature of accounting change both in public sector organizations and generally.

7. Employing a theory that explicitly acknowledges and diagrams the interplay between subjects, tools and tasks _____ (提供新的见解) the design decision-making process, particularly the significance of tool mediation for the realization of tasks during design work.

8. _____ (这个框架已经被证明是有用的) in improving the European structure of the case company. This is a notable and promising side-effect of the exploratory study, at least from a managerial point of view.

Task 12 Revise the following English abstracts.

1. **Abstract**: ① By constructing the RV-GERT network model transferred with n-dimensional random variable, joint distribution function of random variables on directed branches and marginal distribution function of each variable are connected by using a multivariate Copula function in n-dimensional space, the joint probability density function of the random variables then can be deduced. ② The concept of moment generating function (m.g.f.) of multi-dimensional random is proposed. ③ By means of signal flow-graphs theory, the equivalent topological relations are analyzed, and analytical algorithm of RV-GERT network is designed by using Mason formula and characteristics of m.g.f. ④ By implementing equivalent conversions of transmit variable, m.g.f. and W-function, the basic parameters in RV-GERT network such as probability, expectation, variance and relative risk are solved, so as to extend the application range of GERT theory. ⑤ The case researches the development cycle, product weight and battery power time of a new data recording device developed by a commercial aircraft Co., Ltd, and uses the

analytic algorithm of RV-GERT network to inverse the parameters, which shows the science and practicability of the new model.

2. **Abstract**: ① Reaching law control method can improve the dynamic performance of the sliding mode motion. ② This paper for traditional index reaching law has some defects, puts forward a kind of method of exponential approach law based on time-varying handover gain. ③ Current sliding mode controller design for permanent magnet synchronous motors, joined in a switch gain correction factor, makes switching gain during reaching movements and approaches the sliding mode can keep small value and sliding stage with convergence system state. ④ The state equation is established in the controller model, and the sliding mode surface, reaching law was designed. ⑤ Furthemore, it has introduced the derivation process of control law in detail. ⑥ Finally, the rationality and validity of the design is verified by simulation experiment.

Keys to Exercises

Unit 1

Task 1 Read a paper of your field and write the outline of the paper.

略.

Task 2 Read the following sentences and replace the underlined words with academic words.

1. conducted
2. differentiation
3. issue
4. significant
5. concerns

Task 3 Turn the following common words into more academic ones.

help	assist, facilitate, guide, direct
improve	enhance, upgrade, elevate
usually	normally, typically, generally
suitable	appropriate, adequate
whole	complete, entire, comprehensive

Task 4 Find the appropriate academic words for the following phrases.

1. carry out—implement/execute/promulgate/conduct
2. get rid of—eliminate
3. look at carefully—examine
4. look into—investigate
5. find out—discover

Keys to Exercises

6. a lot of—numerous, myriad
7. make sure—ensure/assure
8. be made up of—consist of / comprise / be composed of
9. make clear—elucidate/clarify

Task 5 Read the following sentences and underline the nominalized words.

1. Upon <u>substitution</u> of the actual magnitudes, v turned out to be the velocity of light.
2. All airfields in the country would be nationalized, and the government would continue with the <u>development</u> of new aircraft as recommended by the Brabazon Committee.
3. This is reflected in our <u>admiration</u> for people who have made something of their lives, sometimes against great odds, and in our somewhat disappointed <u>judgment</u> of those who merely drift through life.
4. Researchers have to judge the <u>validity</u> and <u>reliability</u> of the web sites.
5. The <u>possibility</u> of increasing dollar receipts was coupled with a <u>belief</u> that Africa could be a strategic centre for British power.
6. Depending on how unique (or unorthodox) the new method is, its <u>validation</u> probably should be established in a separate publication, published prior to <u>submission</u> of the main study.

Task 6 Turn the following words into nominalized words.

discover	discovery
impair	impairment
allow	allowance
refuse	refusal
propose	proposal
indicate	indication
remove	removal
intend	intention
liable	liability
negligent	negligence
extensive	extension
legal	legality
careless	carelessness
proficient	proficiency

Task 7 Compare the following two texts and pay attention to their differences.

略.

Task 8 Improve the following sentences into more concise ones.

1. The tissue was minced and samples incubated.
2. These experiments showed that samples had evidently been overheated.
3. Dr. Smith suggested postponing the test.
4. The new equipment has been installed.
5. Our preliminary report described the techniques used to infuse fluid into the cerebral ventricles of rats.

Task 9 Write quotations according to the information given below.

1. Humphrey (1959) insisted that "dancers love to suffer, and while they wallow in tragedy, they alienate and bore their audiences" (p. 40).
2. "The main purpose of a dictionary is to prevent or at last reduce communication conflicts which may arise from lexical deficit" (Hartmann, 1987, p. 21).
3. According to Jones (1998), "Students often had diﬁculty using APA style, especially when it was their first time" (p. 100).
4. Jones's (1998) study found the following:

   Students often had difficulty using APA style, especially when it was their first time citing sources. This difficulty could be attributed to the fact that many students failed to purchase a style manual or to ask their teacher for help. (p. 100)

Task 10 Write in-text citations with the information given below.

1. APA style is a difficult citation format for first-time learners. (Jones, 1998)

   Or: According to Jones (1998), APA style is a difficult citation format for first-time learners.
2. Breen and Maassen (2005) conducted a two-phase research project, that firstly explored student perceptions of plagiarism and then developed learning materials to be embedded within courses.
3. Stoleman and O'Connor (1986) argue that it is better for a writer to discuss a narrow aspect of a large topic in detail than to attempt to discuss loose generalizations (p. 4).
4. Barker et al. (1991) investigated the difficulties faced by visited Asian students at Australian universities and suggest that schemes that help to provide friendship and informal skills training will be beneficial to the newly arrived student.

Keys to Exercises

5. It has been suggested by Furnham and Bochner (1986) that practical culture learning experiences can relieve some of the distress experienced by individuals adapting to a new cultural environment.

6. In many disciplines, portions and learning by providing portraits of students, offering multidimensional perspectives, encouraging students to participate, and linking teaching (O'Malley & Valdez Pierce, 1996; Genesee & Upshur, 1996).

Task 11 Make correction to the following reference list.

References

Abel, S. E., Fox, P. T. & Posner, J. P. (1998). Positron emission tomographic studies of the cortical anatomy of single word processing. *Nature*, 331, 585 – 589.

Abel, S. E., Fox, P. T. & Potley, J. R. (1997). Insights from recent positron emission tomographic studies of drug abuse and dependence. *Current Opinion in Psychiatry*, 19(3), 246 – 252.

Balagura, S. (1968). Influence of osmotic and caloric loads upon lateral hypothalamic self-stimulation. *Journal of Comparative and Physiological Psychology*, 66, 325 – 328.

Codon, D. E. (1994, January 10). Kids growing up scared. *Newsweek*, 73, 43 – 49.

Klatzky, R. L. (1980). *Human Memory: Structures and Processes* (2nd ed.). San Francisco: Friedman.

Swaminathan, N. (2007). *Eating Disorders*. Retrieved November 13, 2007, from http://psychologytoday.com/conditions/eating.html.

(APA style exercise-Reference list)

Unit 2

Task 1 Read the following sentences and draw sentence trees as Sample 1 and 2.

1.

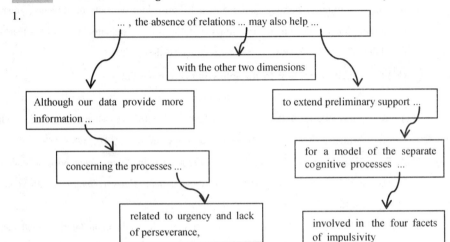

2.

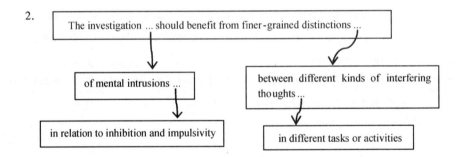

Keys to Exercises

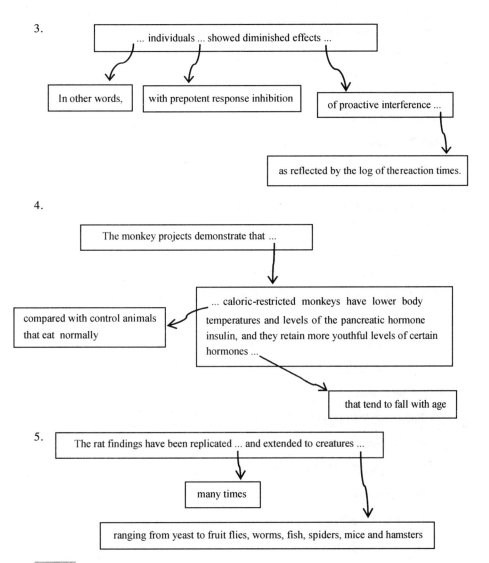

Task 2 Complete the following sentences by translating the Chinese in the brackets into English.

1. the credibility of experimental results
2. the writing of the methods be clear and orderly to avoid confusion and ambiguity
3. the introduction of any novel method for measuring a variable
4. it provides the information the reader needs to judge the study's validity
5. as well as descriptions of unimportant details

6. provide an answer for the research question

7. if necessary, described in more detail in the discussion section

8. the degree to which its outcomes can be attributed to

9. to find a clustering method which is suitable for all types of datasets

10. are different from the objects within other clusters

Task 3 Translate the following sentences into English.

1. What most companies and workforces need are not robots, but creative people who can contribute ideas.

2. And mentally if kids spend too much time living in a virtual world, they may lose the ability to make friends and socialize in a normal way.

3. While governments must no doubt create ecofriendly policy and do their part to bring about change, we as individuals have a crucial role to play as well.

Task 4 The following are English titles of some research papers. Identify the headword of each NP and translate them into Chinese.

1. A Collaborative Filtering Recommendation Algorithm Based on Item Rating Prediction
   基于项目评分预测的协同过滤推荐算法

2. Self-localization systems and algorithms for wireless sensor networks
   无线传感网络中的自身定位系统和算法

3. Multiple faults fuzzy diagnosis for complicated system based on grey theory
   复杂系统多故障灰色模糊诊断技术研究

4. Detection probability calculation and performance evaluation of single pulse radar
   单脉冲雷达检测概率计算及性能评估

5. Database design of information quality inspection system for geoinformation products
   面向地理产品信息化质检系统数据库设计

6. Deformation prediction of grey neural network based on modified fruit fly algorithm
   改进型果蝇算法优化的灰色神经网络变形预测

7. Identity recognition based on improved phase congruency of gait energy image
   基于步态能量图改进的相位一致性特征的身份识别方法

8. Polymorphic ant colony clamping planning based on the machining operation unit

Keys to Exercises

基于加工操作单元的多态蚁群装夹规划方法

9. An optimized deep learning algorithm of convolutional neural network

    一种优化的卷积神经网络深度学习算法

10. Wavelet entropy denoising algorithm of electrocadiogram signals based on correlation

    基于相关性的小波熵心电信号去噪算法

11. Reinforcement learning algorithm for path following control of articulated vehicle

    无人驾驶铰接式车辆强化学习路径跟踪控制算法

12. Multi-objective optimization of hybrid electrical vehicle based on immune genetic algorithm

    免疫遗传算法的混合动力汽车多目标优化

Task 5 Translate the following phrases into English.

1. the focus of public concern
2. environmental problems such as greenhouse gas emissions
3. the climbing unemployment rate
4. the lack of infrastructure and government funding in rural areas
5. an adverse impact on children's mental arithmetic

Task 6 Read the following sentences and underline the NPs and circle the headword in each NPs.

1. Women's immune (response) to allergens weakens with each successive pregnancy.

2. A good (source) of information which can be found on the Internet is the online journal *Science Direct*.

3. Thus, the (tasks) used in this study to evaluate prepotent response inhibition and resistance to proactive interference may be of primary (interest) for the laboratory assessment of cognitive aspects related to distinct facets of impulsivity, namely (urgency and the lack) of perseverance, respectively.

4. The (dissociation) of inhibitory function related to urgency and the (lack) of perseverance may shed some light on certain (processes) involved in some psychopathological conditions.

5. As for sensation seeking, the (absence) of any relationship with inhibition in this study or with decision-making processes, as shown in a previous one (Zermatten et al., 2005), may

underscore the (fact) that this facet of impulsivity is not related to executive control.

6. It is noteworthy that as predicted in our hypothesis, the (lack) of premeditation and sensation seeking were found to be unrelated to (inhibition performances), which indicates that these two dimensions may depend on other psychological processes.

7. The average (distance) travelled to their "main" store by the 276 respondents who switched to the new store, fell by 2.25 kms in the pre-intervention period to 0.98 kms in the post-intervention period.

8. Judging the external (validity) of a study involving human subjects requires that descriptive data be provided regarding the basic (demographic profile) of the sample population, including age, gender, and possibly the racial composition of the sample.

9. Theory and research in psychology show that (a thorough understanding) of an individual's view of an issue or problem is (an essential requirement) for successful change of that person's attitudes and behaviour.

10. (University policy) on academic integrity/misconduct defines (the behaviours) that all stakeholders must abide by, and the (parameters) for reporting, investigating and penalising infringements.

Task 7 Fill in the blanks with the proper verb form.

1. are   2. show
3. is   4. is
5. are   6. is
7. asks   8. include
9. have been considered   10. were not applied

Task 8 Fill in the blanks with proper pronouns.

1. its 2. their 3. its 4. their, he or she 5. their

Task 9 Read the following sentences and underline the coordinate or subordinate construction of each sentence.

1. Finally, a possible framework for understanding the impacts of tourism on health and their interrelationships has been identified. (coordination of sentences)

Keys to Exercises

2. Scientists have studied poison ivy infection for centuries, but they have found no preventive pills or inoculation. (coordination of sentences)
3. On the other hand, some cohorts do not represent the entire patient distribution, which often leads to bad base metric. (subordination)
4. Given these two definitions, both homogeneous and heterogeneous neighborhoods are constructed for all patients in the training data. (coordination of words)
5. In particular, the homogeneous neighborhood of the index patient is the set of retrieved patients that are close in distance measure to the index patient and are also considered similar by the physician. (coordination of phrases)
6. It will never be known how and when this numeration ability developed, but it is certain that numeration was well developed by the time humans had formed even semi-permanent settlements. (coordination of sentences, subordination)
7. We formulate the problem as a supervised metric learning problem, where physician input is used as the supervision information. (subordination)
8. Finally, we demonstrated the use cases through a clinical decision support prototype and quantitatively compared the proposed methods against baselines, where significant performance gain is obtained. (coordination of phrases)
9. We construct features from longitudinal sequences of observable measures based on demographics, medication, lab, vital signs and symptoms. (coordination of words)
10. The second and the third techniques address other related challenges of using such a supervised metric, namely how to update the learned similar metric with new evidence efficiently and how to combine multiple physicians' opinions. (coordination of words and phrases)

Task 10 Read the following sentences and fill in the blanks with proper conjunctions.

1. and
2. but
3. and
4. that
5. which
6. and
7. and
8. and
9. and
10. that

Unit 3

Task 1 Find out the topic sentence, supporting sentences and concluding sentence (if there is any) of each paragraph.

1.

```
         topic sentence ①
          ↗           ↖
supporting        supporting
 sentence          sentence
    ②                ③
          ↘           ↙
       concluding sentence ④
```

2.

```
         topic sentence ①
          ↗           ↖
supporting        supporting
 sentence          sentence
    ②                ③
          ↘           ↙
       concluding sentence ④
```

3.

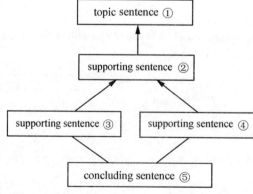

Keys to Exercises

4.
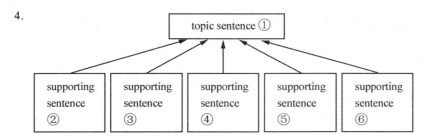

Task 2 Read the following information about "Brain Size and Intelligence". Rearrange the sentences and write a paragraph with the information.

3, 2, 7, 4, 1, 6, 8, 5

Task 3 Read the following sentences and underline the controlling idea in each sentence.

1. Pollution <u>has become a serious problem about which we worry</u>.

2. Somatic cell enhancement engineering <u>should not be performed because it would be morally precarious.</u>

3. Some language loss, like species loss, <u>is natural and predictable.</u>

4. Repressive language policies <u>are common in many parts of the world.</u>

5. Synonyms, words that have the same basic meaning, <u>do not always have the same emotional meaning.</u>

Task 4 Compare the following two paragraphs which discuss the same topic and choose the one that is unified.

Paragraph 1 is unified, while the second one is not.

Task 5 Read the following paragraphs, and decide which pattern each belongs to.

1. Simple Linear Pattern

It is apparent, (T1) / therefore, that universities can benefit from learning about their own students' perceptions of plagiarism in order to develop appropriate strategies to promote academic integrity (R1). In light of this, (T2 = R1) / the aim of our research program is to systematically examine students' understandings of, and attitudes towards, plagiarism, with the intention of informing the institution on approaches that might promote a greater awareness of plagiarism and, therefore, prevent its occurrence (R2). This study (T3 = R2) / is exploratory in nature and will form part of a larger investigation (R3).

```
     T1—R1
       |
     T2 (=R1)—R2
           |
         T3 (=R2)—R3
               |
             Tn (Rn-1)—Rn
```

2. Constant TP

The plant (T1) / is also influenced by other living things with which it competes (R1). It (T2 = T1) / has to withstand parasites, hungry birds, and grazing or gnawing mammals (R2). Yet a plant (T3 = T1) often needs animals to spread its pollen or scatter its seeds (R3).

```
T1—R1
 |
T2 (=T1)—R2
 |
T3 (=T1)—R3
 |
Tn (=T1)—Rn
```

3. Concentrated TP

Albert Einstein, one of the world's geniuses (T1),/ failed in his university entrance examination on his first attempt (R1). William Faulkner, one of America's noted writers (T2),/ never finished college because he could not pass his English courses (R2). Sir Winston Churchill, who is considered one of the masters of the English language (T3),/ had to have special tutoring in English during elementary school (R3). These few examples (T4)/show that failure in school does not always predict failure in life (R4).

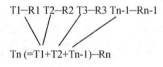

4. Derived TP

My father's face (T1)/ is rough (R1). His complexion (T2 = part of T1)/ is leathery and wrinkled (R2). His nose, broken twice in his life, (T3 = part of T1)/ makes him look like a boxer who has lost too many fights (R3). His mouth, unless he smiles, (T4 = part of T1) looks hard and threatening (R4). His chin (T5 = part of T1) is massive and angular (R5).

Keys to Exercises

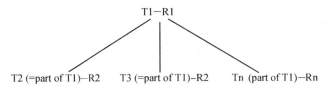

5. Crossing TP

Urbanization (T1) / is a relatively new global issue (R1). As recently as 1950 (T2 = R1), / only 30% of the world's population was urbanized (R2 = T1). Today (T3 = T2), / more than half live in urban centers (R3 = R2).

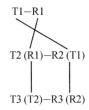

Task 6 Rearrange the following sentences to make logical paragraphs.

1. 1), 4), 3), 2)
2. 3), 2), 4), 1)

Task 7 Fill in the blanks with the information given in the brackets.

1. These plants   The pigments
2. A total of 41 students   Each focus group
3. One objection   public transport
4. This approach

Task 8 Read the following paragraphs and underline the logical connectors.

1. There are roughly three New Yorks. There is, <u>first</u>, the New York of the man or woman who was born here, who takes the city for granted and accepts its size and its turbulence as natural and inevitable. <u>Second</u>, there is the New York of the commuter—the city that is devoured by locusts each day and spat out each night. <u>Third</u>, there is the New York of the person who was born somewhere else and came to New York in quest of something. <u>Of these three trembling cities</u> the greatest is the last—the city of final destination, the city that is a goal. It is this third city that accounts for New York's high-strung disposition, its poetical deportment, its dedication to the arts, and its incomparable achievements. Commuters give the city its tidal restlessness; natives give it solidity and continuity; but settlers give it passion.

2. Great efforts were made to improve the fermentation yield of streptomycin. Some of its major metabolic precursors were isolated and identified some times ago. Recently, the biosynthesis pathways of streptomycin and its genetic control were described. In addition to biosynthetic pathways, fermentation conditions were studied to improve production yield. The use of batch-type feeding of carbohydrates resulted in an production yield. The use of batch-type feeding of carbonhydrates resulted in an increase of yield by 23%~24%. Moreover, the effects of carbon source consumption rate on streptomycin production were investigated. The yield when 34 g·L^{-1} of olive oil was used as the sole carbon source is about 2.0-fold higher than when starch medium was used. (张俊东, 2018, p.70)

3. In this study, we report that G protein promotes lung cancer cell invasion. Moreover, we demonstrate that inhibition of G protein reduces the metastasis of lung cancer cells in vivo. Finally, we demonstrate that the expression of G protein is significantly up-regulated in the early stages of lung cancer. (张俊东, 2018, p.74)

Task 9 Fill in the gaps in the paragraphs below to see how the paragraphs is logically connected.

(1) But, Thus, However

(2) However, Moreover, Finally, for example

Unit 4

Task 1 Read and outline the following passage.

Outline:

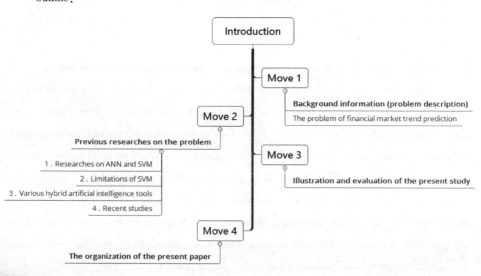

Keys to Exercises

Task 2 Fill in the blanks with the information in the brackets.

1. have drawn an increasing attention
2. more and more technical fields have begun
3. has heightened the need for computational tools
4. have been used as
5. has received due attention
6. has long been associated with
7. One of the most controversial issues
8. Much research in recent years has focused on
9. are an important and useful element
10. there has been growing interest

Task 3 Translate the following sentences into English.

1. In the past 30 years, there has been a steady increase in the use of student evaluation of instruction.
2. The budget has historically played center stage in most organizations' systems of management control.
3. In recent decades there has been an enormous increase in the range of tasks to which computers have been applied.
4. Math education has been an important part of education for the growing number of students from different cultures attending U.S. schools.
5. Concern about global warming and urban air pollution has become central issues in transport policy decision-making.

Task 4 Fill in the blanks with the information in the brackets.

1. ① A number of research studies have been conducted to investigate
   ② have developed
   ③ noted
   ④ claim
2. ① a great body of research has been devoted to examine
   ② early studies; produced contradictory results
   ③ have attributed these discrepant findings in part to
   ④ proposed
   ⑤ several instruments have been developed and widely adopted to measure

Task 5 The sentences in each paragraph are not presented in their correct order. Number the sentences in a logical order.

1.

There is general agreement that computers will continue to enjoy a central place in education. Jevons (1990) and Smart (1995) forecast increasing access to and use of computers in schools. Schmidt (1982) identified three uses in the classroom: as the object of a course, as a means of support, and as a means of providing instruction. Green and Barnes (1991) cite a number of specific applications in the training of accountancy students ranging from drills to simulation exercises.

2.

The majority of English coursebooks in China provide students with long lists of vocabulary attached to the end of the texts. Since vocabulary is regarded as central to language learning, students are supposed to memorise all the new words and expressions on which they will be tested. Teachers rarely consider which items may be students' active vocabulary and which items may be students' passive vocabulary. Therefore, they treat all the new words and expressions with an equal amount of time and care, and students tend to treat all the new items as active vocabulary.

Task 6 Translate the following sentences into Chinese.
1. 然而,这些试验只进行了2~3年的平均随访,无法证明对大肠癌有任何影响。
2. 然而,这些试图在二手烟和肺癌之间建立联系的尝试目前仍有争议。
3. 然而,双酚和树胶的共聚物目前还没有作为医用植入物进行研究。
4. 然而,这两个研究都没有提供任何描述性的证据,说明句子衔接词在学术文本中的实际位置。
5. 不幸的是,目前对于关节软骨修复的治疗方案有一定的局限性。

Task 7 Translate the following parts in the brackets into English.
1. was not fully established
2. the previously mentioned methods suffer from some limitations
3. has been investigated extensively, was obtained, cannot be controlled
4. have been widely investigated, but few practical applications

Task 8 Translate the following parts in the brackets into English.
1. The present work extends the use of the last model to; In addition, an effort is made to improve

2. The purpose of this research was to further investigate and characterize

3. In this paper, we propose an alternative distributed approach

Task 9 Translate the following into Chinese.

1. 在本文中,我们对十二篇发表的文章样本中的句子连接词位置作了初步研究报告。

2. 本研究采用新的方法研究学术写作任务,试图对这些问题提供一些初步的答案,希望其他研究者能以此为起点。

3. 基于学习者对一种语言的态度可能影响他们学习这种语言的假设,本文报告了一项考察中国学生对新加坡英语态度的研究。

Task 10 Read the following paragraphs to see how the paper is organized.

略。

Unit 5

Task 1 Read and outline methods section.

Outline:

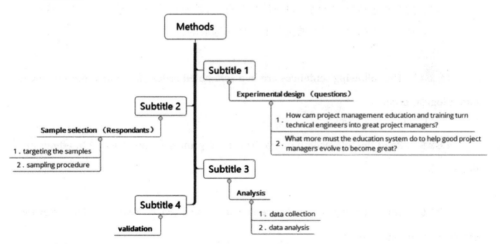

Task 2 Translate the following sentences into English.

1. The experiment was initiated to investigate the perceptions of English needs in a medical context among college students in China.

2. The investigation was performed in a national laboratory affiliated to a research center for industrial automation in Shanghai.

3. The aim of this study is to confirm that the computer dictionary would increase learners look-up behavior more than the paper dictionary as found in the previous comparison studies.

4. Two studies were conducted at a southwestern university with undergraduate students ranging from 19- to 22-year-old, majoring in fields other than Spanish.

5. In order to investigate the research question, a quantitative research design was employed in this study, which was aimed at exploring the correlation between the concerned variables.

Task 3 Translate the following paragraphs into Chinese.

1. 我们所采用的定性方法使我们能够收集到大量的信息:(1)学生对其英语写作的发展的看法;(2)学生对不是英语写作而是与写作课程参与有关的其他成果或"副产品"的看法;(3)教师对学生在写作课程中的变化的观察。

2. 这项研究分两个阶段进行,目的是首先从 IT 招聘者的角度,找出成功聘用有效项目经理最常见的特点。一旦确定了这些特征,该研究试图从全国范围内的 IT 企业高管的角度来确定这些特征的偏好。

3. 目前的调查包括对六个地点进行取样和分析,以测量地下水化学的变化。这些地点是从位于英格兰东南部的伦敦盆地地区选取的,这个地区经常被用来解释地下水的演变。

Task 4 The following sentences are in a scrambled order. Rearrange the sentences into a logical order.

4 3 2 6 5 1

Task 5 Read the following paragraphs carefully and see how research methods are described.

略.

Task 6 The following sentences are in a scrambled order. Rearrange the following sentences into logical order.

3 4 1 5 6 2

Task 7 Translate the following paragraphs into Chinese.

1. 中国英语专业的三组学生参加了本研究。之所以只招收英语专业的学生,是因为担心如果不这样做,他们可能没有足够的英语写作经验,无法提供有关他们写作焦虑经历的丰富信息。

Keys to Exercises

2. 所有受试者都是拉夫堡大学的国际研究生。选择受试者的标准是,他们以前没有在英国居住或访问超过两个星期,也不是欧盟的国民,也不是以英语为母语的人。

3. 参与者有40位家长:21位新来的中国移民和19位来自不同家庭的非移民加拿大白人。这些家庭总共有46个孩子,21个中国人和25个欧洲裔加拿大人。只有一名父亲参加了面谈,只有一个家庭让父母双方参加面谈;其余家庭由母亲代表。这些家庭居住在一个中等规模的加拿大都市。来自台湾、大陆和香港的中国家庭在过去10年内移民到加拿大,其中大多数人(18人)在过去5年内移民到加拿大。非移民家庭的成员都是白人,出生在加拿大,一直居住在加拿大。

Task 8 Read the following excerpts taken from experimental papers and decide which part of method they belong to.

1. Participants 2. Participants 3. Sample selection 4. Subjects

Task 9 Read the following paragraph and see how research materials are described.
略。

Task 10 Translate the following parts in the brackets into English.

1. consisted of thirteen 5-point Likert scale questions
2. multiple-choice tests were prepared
3. used structured interviewing
4. A case-study approach was adopted
5. Of the 15 criteria identified

Task 11 Underline the research materials or instruments used in the following sentences.

1. <u>A 32-item questionnaire</u> was mailed to 3,258 IT managers and executives, asking them, through a <u>7-point Likert scale</u>, to identify the relative importance of each of the 15 criteria in their screening of PM candidates for their organizations.

2. The substrate used in the present study was <u>chromium coated sodalime glass slides</u>, because cadmium and zinc were found to stick poorly over glass.

3. <u>A multiple-choice test</u> which can measure the receptive knowledge of the words was considered appropriate to measure the retention of the words gained incidentally from reading, since the probability that the participants can gain word knowledge at the production level at one exposure is very low. The immediate test and the delayed test contained the same items, but in a scrambled order.

4. <u>The two-page response sheet</u> (see Appendix C) was adapted from Kayaer & Bhundhumani

(2007). Each participant received an identical response sheet to record his or her responses to the same questions for both stimuli. The response sheet included questions regarding each woman's estimated weight and asked participants to rate the woman's weight based on her height being either 63 in (1.6 m) or 67 in (1.7 m). The researchers asked participants to rate their perception of the women's levels of happiness and success in life. The response sheet asked participants to judge how popular, friendly, judgmental and outgoing each woman was. The researchers added additional questions regarding how often the participants thought the women dieted and exercised.

Task 12 Read the following paragraph and underline the research procedures.

<u>In the main session</u>, the participants of the paper group were provided with Sisa Elite English-Korean dictionaries in the classroom. <u>Meanwhile</u>, the participants of the computer group participated in the experiment in a computer lab where they could access the same version of the dictionary through the computer. <u>First</u>, the students were instructed to read the printed text for a comprehension test. The vocabulary test was not announced so that the condition was conducive to incidental vocabulary learning. There was no time limit, but they were advised to read the text within 15 minutes. They were allowed to consult dictionaries as much as they needed. However, they were asked to underline the words they looked up in the dictionary. <u>After they finished their reading</u>, the reading comprehension test was administered. <u>Then</u>, an unannounced vocabulary test was given. <u>Finally</u>, the participants were asked to respond to the questionnaire. <u>Two days after the main session</u>, a delayed unannounced vocabulary test was given in the presence of the researcher.

Task 13 Translate the following sentences into Chinese.

1. 实验包括预试、主试和延迟试验。所有这些课程均于2003年5月在正常上课时间内和在正常教室举行,并由一名负责这两个班的教员协助。
2. 阅读文本之前,在研究者在场的情况下,使用前置测试来测量目标单词的预知量。基于结果,超过90%的受访者不知道的14个目标词被选中。

Task 14 Translate the following Chinese in the brackets into English.

Each of the 773 essays <u>was transcribed</u>(转录) by the researcher for use with the CLAN computer program (MacWhinney, 1995). <u>This program is normally used</u>(这个程序通常用于) for the analysis of spoken child language, but <u>the transcription system</u>(这个转录系统) was adapted for written texts according to the suggestions in the CLAN manual. The essays were transcribed using standard orthography.

Keys to Exercises

After the transcriptions were complete(转录完成后), the program was used to tag the lexical category and morphological inflections of each word. The mean length of the essays is 175 words (S. D. 88.4). During the first stage of the tagging process(在标记过程的第一个阶段), the program assigned likely codes for each item. The texts were then(然后) handchecked by the researcher for mistakes in the machine coding and ambiguous items such as WH words, which can be interrogative pronouns, relative pronouns or adverbial clause markers.

Task 15 Fill in the blanks with the proper forms of the given words.

1. were scored; was given
2. was read; were found; were identified and grouped
3. was constructed, named and defined; was done
4. were computer-analyzed; were determined; were conducted

Unit 6

Task 1 The following is the discussion part of one paper. Read and pay attention to the functions of different parts.

In this paper we have presented two methods (EML and EML +) to suppress the forgetting of unused classes in an online incremental learning setup. Since the classes of data in a real-time online stream are not necessarily uniformly distributed, they can create a block of absence. During this absence, an unused class is not learned and the model is prone to forget it. Our methods use competitive updates in traditional RLS that focus on the importance of the data points in the stream during the learning process. This shrinks the blocks of absence of a class while keeping the important information available for the learning process. (Commenting on the method the study used)

We compared our techniques using four baseline models and achieved better results than the baseline techniques. We discuss several options for incremental learning, some of which have been used for online or incremental handwriting recognition. As we wanted to show the usability of the proposed models not only for handwriting recognition, but also for various other problems, we chose to test a spectrum of datasets. We evaluated results on 8 datasets that varied in the number of classes, features and sample sizes. In all of the applications our techniques achieved a good trade-off between the immunity for forgetting of unused classes and the general accuracy of the model. (Summarizing the major results)

From the results we can see that both of our methods are superior to the original RLS in regard to the immunity to forgetting of the unused classes, and they both are capable of maintaining the general accuracy of the models. The general accuracy is very important for the model to be able to achieve good results even when there are no blocks of absence of classes, and our methods do not influence the learning process of all the other classes. In some rare cases, however, the general accuracy was lower than in the original models. We believe that this is due to the nature of the data and the importance of each sample for the learning process. The learning process of all classes is slightly slowed down compared to a case in which all classes are learned at the same time. Especially in EML, the learning is more competitive than in EML +. This follows our assumption, since by using more samples in EML + we were able to improve the general accuracy of the model. Further we point out that if we focus on the last samples' accuracy, the results improve as well. This corresponds to our theory that worse results are caused by lack of data due to the competitive nature of the model. On the other hand, the more competitive the learning is, the more it is, in general, immune to forgetting. Again, there are some rare cases when this is not completely true; but since in both EML and EML + the learning is competitive, we can see that using such learning is superior to learning all samples, as in RLS. We can note that in all cases our methods surpassed RLS and in the vast majority of the results the improvement was very significant. (Discussing the major findings)

Given these findings we can state that our approaches outperform baseline techniques significantly in cases where some classes are used only on rare occasions compared to the rest of the classes. This gain in performance is reduced when distribution over classes is more or less uniform. However, this reduction is not critical and both methods lead to comparable or even superior results when there are no blocks of absence of classes present. Nevertheless, the main application of our models is on handwritten gestures recognition. Consequently, we might suppose that the distribution of handwritten gestures of users in a real-world setting is not uniform and that several gestures are used only on rare occasions. (Drawing conclusion and giving implication)

In our future work we want to explore the problem of forgetting in cases where even though our methods did indeed improve the original results, the accuracy during the forgetting phase was still not acceptable. It might seem that for these datasets either the models or the competitive learning process itself is not quite suitable. As a part of this research we want to investigate the application of our EML and EML + to optimization techniques other than RLS. (Raising questions for the future research)

Keys to Exercises

Task 2 Complete the following sentences according to the Chinese in the brackets.

1. showed a tendency to increase
2. decreased rapidly
3. a 16% drop
4. was much lower in 2003 than in 2001
5. whereas
6. was closely related to
7. The coefficient of correlation
8. is consistent with
9. match with
10. 90 subjects

Task 3 Translate the following sentences into English.

1. Thirty-two individuals returned the questionnaires.
2. Nearly one third of participants prefer to go online with a smart phone.
3. Age was highly correlated with experience for workers in skilled jobs.
4. The value does not agree with the standard value.
5. Prices showed a tendency to increase over the past three years.

Task 4 Translate the following sentences into Chinese.

1. 所得的石蜡、冰和铅含量与公布值一致。
2. 结果表明,这两种汽车的油耗和可靠性有明显差异。除两个例外情况外,A 牌车子始终比平均数更经济、更可靠,而 B 牌车子则比平均数更不可靠,只有三个例外情况。
3. 如图所示,电视销售呈上升趋势。今年 2 月,电视销量从 1200 台上升到 1400 台。在 3 月份,它们保持在 1400 台不变。在接下来的两个月里,它们稳步增长,从 1400 台增加到 1800 台。然而,在接下来的两个月里,它们稳步下跌,8 月份又回到了 1200 台。在这次急剧的下跌之后,接下来的几个月电视销量大幅上升,去年 12 月电视销量上升到 2200 台。
4. 图 1.1 显示非沉浸式和沉浸式英语学生的四项测验的分数。参加英语沉浸课程的学生的成绩明显好于没有参加四个现代语言协会考试的学生。
5. 美国严重的健康成本问题可以从表 1 中看出,美国的健康服务成本与其他几个国家相比。正如我们从表中看到的,美国的数字几乎是第二高成本日本的两倍,而且比所有其他发达国家或发展中国家都要高得多。

Task 5 Read the following passages and decide the functions of each paragraph.

1. Explaining the possible reasons
2. Evaluating the significance of a result
3. Interpreting the major finding
4. Interpreting the major finding
5. Discussing the limitations of the research
6. Restating the purpose of the research and discussing the implications of the research
7. Discussing the implications of the research
8. Making conclusion

Task 6 Complete the following sentences according to the Chinese in the brackets.

1. indicated
2. perhaps because
3. are understandable
4. It was conjectured
5. agree well with
6. are consistent with
7. are crucial for
8. Compared to
9. In agreement with
10. Limitations of this approach

Task 7 Translate the following sentences into Chinese.

1. 分析结果表明,最重要的可持续性标准是与行为相关的标准,其次是商业因素。在这些行为标准中,伦理、竞争情报、内在动机和自我效能感尤为重要。
2. 几种不同的损伤机理,如磨损、塑性变形和滚动接触疲劳,可能是造成车轮不圆和钢轨波磨的原因。
3. 这些结果表明,与未受过训练的章鱼相比,通过观察其他章鱼的行为而不是通过奖励和惩罚的方法,可以更快地学会一项任务。
4. 通过对这两种粘着力模型的仿真结果与实验结果的比较,发现这些粘着力模型能够有效地反映实验结果。
5. 专家的观点可能受到其职业道路、学术培训或经验产生的偏见的影响。然而,这也是这种方法的优点,它是基于不同文化背景下有经验的人的观点。

Keys to Exercises

6. 我们的发现支持了此前在英国和荷兰的研究,证实了目前的药物分类系统与损害证据几乎没有关系。他们也同意以前专家报告的结论,积极针对酒精危害是一个有效的和必要的公共卫生战略。

Task 8　Read the following sentences and underline the tentative words and phrases used.

1. If this latter trend were to follow that of government health costs, the trend <u>would be</u> approximately given by the dotted line portion of curve b in the figure.

2. <u>It is likely that</u> such severe turbulence affected the automatic landing indicators which had failed or displayed faulty data during descent to the Toledo airport.

3. The final judgment of the matter <u>may be</u> difficult or impossible because of the lack of good test data that could be obtained from other portions of the severely damaged aircraft.

4. In the case of building roads connecting cities, there <u>might be</u> some costs involved with every road intersection.

5. The weather condition at the time <u>suggests</u> that the most likely cause of the damage to the rudder was due to both vertical and horizontal air turbulence.

6. <u>It is possible</u> of course that other industries with a different complex of speed jobs and skilled jobs <u>may produce</u> entirely different results.

7. Their L1 switching for rhetorical concerns <u>may involve</u> relatively complex and interactive mental operations to explore variables between lexis and context environments in a contrastive rhetorical pattern.

8. However, the repeated L-S in their verbalizations in searching words <u>could be considered as</u> an output condition that in the long term could help them to build an internally associative system between the two languages.

9. Application of simple statistical techniques like interpolation of state/regional level inventories to obtain gridded data <u>is likely to</u> cause misrepresentation of emissions at sub-regional scales, which can get accumulated to the global scale in the models.

10. The location of emission hot spots <u>seems to</u> correlate to the densely populated rural areas, once again emphasizing the contribution of rural bio-fuel emissions.

11. We <u>might have overestimated</u> the latent period duration before an effect of aspirin on death due to colorectal cancer.

12. A similarly large change in the weight on drug-specific damage <u>would be needed</u>, from about 4% to slightly more than 70%, for tobacco to displace alcohol at first position.

And an increase in the weight on harm to users from 46% to nearly 70% <u>would be necessary</u> for crack cocaine to achieve the overall most harmful position.

Task 9 **Below are some statements which may sound too definite. Rewrite them to make them sound more tentative.**

a. Use tentative verbs such as "seem", "appear", "suggest", "tend".

1. In this case, the prediction of accident rates between age groups appears to be confirmed.

2. The HP participants tended to switch from the L2 to their L1 for problem-solving and ideational thinking.

3. The lack of exposure to the target language may be the reason for the students' poor listening ability.

b. Use modal auxiliaries such as "can/could", "may/might", "should".

1. The reasons for this erratic pattern could be the age distribution of the children or the relatively small number of women in the sample.

2. These results can/may be explained by considering the voltage distribution on 230kv insulators during freezing conditions.

3. These discrepancies may be due to lack of purity in the substance.

4. Other variables, for which there are no objective data, may influence the frequency of the outcomes.

5. The amount and type of graphic presentation may reflect the designer's view of potential readers.

Unit 7

Task 1 **Contrast the following abstracts and tell the differences between the descriptive abstract and the informative abstract.**

1. Descriptive abstract

Sentence ① talks about the purpose of the study. Sentence ② is about the content/scope of the study.

2. Informative abstract

Sentence ① briefly summarizes the study. Sentence ② describes the used method. Sentence ③ ⋯ ⑤ presents the principal findings and Sentence ⑥ is the conclusion.

Keys to Exercises

Task 2 Read the following three abstracts and try to figure out what elements are included in these abstracts.

1.

Purpose	① This study investigated …	① research objectives
Method	② Sixty-eight Japanese undergraduate students … in English. ③ Their English lexical proficiency … were assessed.	② the materials used ③ the method used
Results and discussion	④ Multiple regression analysis of the data showed that … ⑤ However … and the length of summaries.	④ results ⑤ discussion
Conclusion	⑥ It is suggested that …	⑥ indications or suggestions

2.

Purpose	① A … controller is designed. ② This model is …	① objectives ② background information
Method	③ … optimal control method is used.	③ the method used
Results and discussion	④ Simulation studies demonstrates that …	④ results and discussion
Conclusion		no

3.

Purpose	① Many … techniques … have proposed, but the inspection intervals … have not been comprehensively addressed. ② The present study focuses on …	① limitations ② objectives
Method	③ Dent sizes are considered … ④ The life-cycle strength … is obtained … ⑤ Maintenance cost is introduced.	③ the materials used ④ and ⑤ the method used
Results and discussion	⑥ This method enables … which facilitate … and adjust …	⑥ results and discussion
Conclusion		no

Task 3 Read the following sentences and decide what function each one has in the abstract.

1. background information
2. background information
3. the purpose of the study
4. the purpose of the study
5. the main content of the study
6. the main content of the study

Task 4 Translate the following underlined parts into Chinese.

1. 论文的目的是探讨
2. 我们已经调查过了
3. 这项研究涉及
4. 这篇论文的重点是
5. 这篇论文探讨了

Task 5 Translate the following Chinese in the brackets into English.

1. The purpose of this report is to discuss
2. This study was conducted to determine
3. This paper develops and tests hypotheses
4. This study aims to assess
5. ① There is little research to link ② This gap in the literature ③ This study is an effort to fill this gap
6. ① Little attention has been given to ② This study develops and tests a model to assess

Task 6 Fill in the blanks with the proper forms of the given words.

1. is required
2. is proposed
3. is described
4. were trained
5. are taken
6. were obtained
7. applied
8. was used

Keys to Exercises

Task 7 Underline the method part of the following abstracts.

1. Growth and Characterization of $Cd_{1-x}Zn_xTe$ Thin Films Prepared from Elemental Multilayer Deposition

Rajiv Ganguly[a], Sumana Hajra[a], Tamosha Mandal[a],

Pushan Banerjeeu[b], Biswait Ghosh[b]

$Cd_{1-x}Zn_xTe$ is key material for fabrication of high-energy radiation detectors and optical devices. Conventionally it is fabricated using single crystal growth techniques. <u>The method adapted here is the deposition of elemental multilayer followed by thermal annealing in vacuum. The multilayer structure was annealed at different temperatures using one to five repetitions of Cd-Zn-Te sequence. X-ray diffraction pattern for the multilayer with five repetitions revealed that annealing at 475°C yielded single-phase material compared to other annealing conditions. EDX spectroscopy was carried out to study the corresponding compositions. Photoluminescence properties and change of resistance of the multilayer under illumination were also studied.</u> The resistivity of the best sample was found to be a few hundreds of Ω cm. (Ganguly et al., 2010, pp. 4879 – 4882)

2. This study explores the relationship between language and communication skills and patterns of success and failure in the cross-cultural adjustment of Japanese university students. <u>Seven interpersonal communication skills which were selected by Ruben and Kealey as important to cross-cultural adjustment were examined: empathy, respect, role behavior flexibility, orientation to knowledge, interaction posture, interaction management, and tolerance for ambiguity. Besides these skills, language was taken into consideration as a major component influencing Japanese intercultural communication. The behavioral assessment method developed by Ruben was utilized to measure communicative performance and behaviors of Japanese university students who visited the United States for 4 weeks for their English training. In order to assess the language skills of these individuals, listening, speaking, structure and written expression, and vocabulary and reading comprehension skills were measured. At the end of their stay in the United States, the dimensions of culture shock, psychological adjustment, and interactional effectiveness were examined.</u> Comparisons of pre- and post-test measures indicated that six out of the seven communication behaviors observed in the Japanese students did not predict success or failure in adjustment to the United States. Only ambiguity tolerance yielded correlation with culture shock. However, speaking and listening skills were closely correlated with interactional effectiveness. (Hiroko, 1985, p. 247)

Task 8 Translate the following sentences into Chinese.

1. 结果表明,写作过程比记笔记更费力。
2. 研究结果表明,不同学习风格学生的听力、写作、结构和阅读平均分存在显著差异。
3. 研究结果表明,人们对使用手机有不同的感受和态度。
4. 研究发现,学生更倾向于使用元认知策略,而情感和记忆策略的使用最少。
5. 研究结果显示,组织学习与财务绩效之间存在显著的、积极的、强有力的关系。
6. 研究结果提出了具体的方法,让教师从学生的文化背景中汲取优势,帮助他们在 L1 和 L2 写作技能之间架起桥梁。

Task 9 Translate the following Chinese in the brackets into English.

1. ANOVA results suggest that
2. Results indicate that
3. These results suggest
4. The results from single language conditions revealed
5. Our findings further suggest
6. The results from case studies support
7. The results demonstrate
8. Findings revealed

Task 10 Translate the following Chinese in the brackets into English.

1. It is concluded
2. This paper concludes that
3. offers practical help
4. serves as a foundation on
5. provides a starting-point for further research
6. provides historical context for
7. offers new insight into
8. The framework has proven to be useful

Task 11 Revise the following English abstracts.

1. ① <u>A RV-GERT network model transferred with n-dimensional random variable is constructed.</u>(研究内容)② With a multivariate Copula function in n-dimensional space, joint distribution function of random variables on directed branches and marginal distribution function of each variable are connected, and the joint probability density function of the random variables is then deduced.(研究方法)③ The paper also defines the concept of moment generating

function(m. g. f.) of multi-dimensional random which is used to design an analytical algorithm of RV-GERT network by means of signal flow-graphs theory and the equivalent topological relations. (研究内容)④ The implementation of equivalent conversions of transmit variable, m. g. f. and W-function indicates that the basic parameter problems in RV-GERT network such as probability, expectation, variance and relative risk can be solved and the application of GERT theory may be extended. (研究结果)⑤ The model was applied to a new data recording device developed by a commercial aircraft Co., Ltd to analyze its development cycle, product weight and battery power time. (研究结果)⑥ By performing parameter inversion with the analytic algorithm of RV-GERT network and comparing with conventional analytical algorithms for single-pass of multiple parameters, the feasibility and practicability of the new model has been proved. (讨论研究意义)

2. ① The reaching law control can improve the sliding mode dynamics. (研究背景)② This paper proposes an index reaching law control method based on a variable switch gain in view of the defects of the conventional way. (主要研究内容)③ A current sliding mode controller was designed for permanent magnet synchronous motors to keep a smaller value of switching gain and convergences during the process of approaching the sliding mode area after a correction factor is added. (研究方法)④ The state equation in the controller model was established, and the sliding mode surface and reaching law were designed as well. (研究结果)⑤ Furthermore, the derivation process of control law was introduced. (研究结果)⑥ The rationality and validity of the design is verified by simulation experiment. (研究意义)

Bibliography

Abernethy, M. A. et al. (2010). Leadership and control system design. *Management Accounting Research*, 21(1), 2–16.

APA style exercise-reference list. (n.d.). Retrieved from http://www.doc88.com/p-9803191129594.html.

Baba, Kyoko. (2009). Aspects of lexical proficiency in writing summaries in a foreign language. *Journal of Second Language Writing*, 18(3), 191–208.

Balat-Pichelin, M. & Bêche, E. (2010). Atomic oxygen recombination on the ODS PM 1000 at high temperature under air plasma. *Applied Surface Science*, 256(16), 4906–4914.

Bao, Yan et al. (2013). Temporal order perception of auditory stimuli is selectively modified by tonal and non-tonal language environments. *Cognition*, 129(3), 579–585.

Chandler, J. (2003). The efficacy of various kinds of error feedback for improvement in the accuracy and fluency of L2 student writing. *Journal of Second Language Writing*, 12(3), 267–296.

Chang, June C. (2005). Faculty-student interation at the community college: A focus on students of color. *Research in Higher Education*, 46, 780.

Chen, Xi, Ren, He & Bil, Cees. (2014). Inspection intervals optimization for aircraft composite structures considering dent damage. *Journal of Aircraft*, 51(1), 303.

Davarynejad, M. et al. (2010). Evolutionary hidden information detection by granulation-based fitness approximation. *Applied Soft Computing*, 10(3), 719–729.

Dudley, W. R. (2002). Learning to make things happen in different ways: Causality in the writing of middle-grade English language learners. *Journal of Second Language Writing*, 11(4), 311–328.

Bibliography

Ganguly, R. et al. Growth and characterization of $Cd_{1-x}Zn_xTe$ thin films prepared from element multilayer deposition. *Applied Surface Science*, 256(16), 4879 – 4882.

Geim, A. K. et al. (2001). Detection of earth rotation with a diamagnetically levitating gyroscope. *Physica B: Condensed Matter*, 294, 739.

Gullifer, J. & Graham, A. (2010). Exploring university students perceptions of plagiarism: A focus group study. *Studies in Higher Education*, 35(4), 463 – 481.

Halliday, M. A. K. (1994). *An Introduction to Functional Grammar (2nd ed.)*. London: Edward Arnold, 94.

Hiroko, Nishida. (1985). Japanese intercultural communication competence and cross-cultural adjustment. *International Journal of Intercultural Relations*, 9(3), 247 – 269.

Kennedy, F. A. & Widener, S. K. (2008). A control framework: Insights from evidence on lean accounting. *Management Accounting Research*, 19(4), 301 – 323.

Manoj, T. & Deepak, K. (2018). A hybrid financial trading support system using multi-category classifiers and random forest. *Applied Soft Computing*, 67, 337 – 349.

Meslinet, E. et al. (2010). Kinetic of solute clustering in neutron irradiated ferritic model alloys and a French pressure vessel steel investigated by atom probe tomography. *Journal of Nuclear Materials*, 399(2 – 3), 137 – 145.

Nutt, David J. et al. (2010). Drug harms in the UK: A multicriteria decision analysis. *The Lancet*, 376(9752), 1558 – 1565.

Radia, P. & Stapleton, P. (2008). Unconventional Internet genres and their impact on second language undergraduate students' writing process. *Internet and Higher Education*, 11(1), 9 – 17.

Rajiv, Ganguly, et al. (2010). Growth and characterization of $Cd_{1-x}Zn_xTe$ thin films prepared from elemental multilayer deposition. *Applied Surface Science*, 256(16), 4879 – 4882.

Ramazani, J. & Jergeas, G. (2015). Project managers and the journey from good to great: The benefits of investment in project management training and education. *International Journal of Project Management*, 33(1), 41 – 52.

Rothwell, Peter M. et al. (2010). Long-term effect of aspirin on colorectal cancer incidence and mortality: 20-year follow-up of five randomised trials. *The Lancet*, 376(9752), 1741 – 1750.

Sua, Caina et al. (2010). Electrochemical behavior of cobalt from 1-butyl-3-methylimidazolium tetrafluoroborate ionic liquid. *Applied Surface Science*, 256(16), 4888 – 4893.

Swales, J. M. & Feak, C. B. (2004). *Academic Writing for Graduate Students*. Ann Arbar: University of Michigan Press/ESL.

Thakur, M. & Kumar, D. (2018). A hybrid financial trading support system using multi-category classifiers and random forest. *Applied Soft Computing*, 67, 337–349.

Wang, Lurong. (2003). Switching to first language among writers with differing second-language proficiency[J]. *Journal of Second Language Writing*, 12(4), 347–375.

Zhao, Lindong & Tang, Shengjing. (2015). Dynamic inverse based controller for a hypersonic flight vehicle. International Conference on Information Sciences, Machinery, Materials and Energy (ICISMME).

丁往道. 英语写作基础教程[M]. 北京：高等教育出版社, 2000.

何康民. 英语学术论文写作[M]. 武汉：武汉大学出版社, 2007.

胡庚申. 英语论文写作与发表[M]. 北京：高等教育出版社, 2008.

刘振聪, 修月祯. 英语学术论文写作[M]. 北京：中国人民大学出版社, 2009.

陆红. 研究生英语写作教程[M]. 苏州：苏州大学出版社, 2011.

杨俊峰. 英语写作基础[M]. 沈阳：辽宁大学出版社, 2003.

庞红梅. 英语研究论文读写教程[M]. 北京：清华大学出版社, 2013.

张德禄, 刘洪民. 主位结构与语篇连贯[J]. 外语研究, 1994(3)：27—33.

张俊东, 杨亲正, 国防. SCI论文写作和发表[M]. 北京：化学工业出版社, 2018.

郑玉琪, 邹长征. 研究生学术英语写作教程[M]. 北京：外语教学与研究出版社, 2015.

钟似璇. 英语科技论文写作与发表[M]. 天津：天津大学出版社, 2004.